Parents Speak Out

Growing With a Handicapped Child

Ann P. Turnbull
H. Rutherford Turnbull III
University of North Carolina, Chapel Hill

Charles E. Merrill Publishing Co.
A Bell & Howell Company
Columbus   Toronto   London   Sydney

9-9-97

Photo on p. 176 from *Newsweek* photographer Robert McElroy.

This book was set in Optima and Ronda.
The production editor was Jan Hall.
The cover was prepared by Jamie Berger.

First Trade Edition Printing, September, 1979

Library of Congress Catalog Card Number: 77–93135

ISBN: O–675–01043–8

Published by
TRADE DIVISION
Charles E. Merrill Publishing Company
A Bell & Howell Company
1300 Alum Creek Drive
Columbus, Ohio 43216

1 2 3 4 5 6 7 8 9 10/85 84 83 82 81 80 79

PRINTED IN THE UNITED STATES OF AMERICA

To Our Children

Preface

In the past decade it has become increasingly popular to identify two major groups of people—parents of handicapped children and professionals. Alliances and confrontations between these two groups have been planned, developed, recorded, or otherwise acted out. In the process we have become insensitive to the fact that many persons are members of both groups. It is possible to be a professional and a parent and vice versa. The majority of professionals are parents, but the majority of parents are not professionals. This book is about professionals who are parents. It is for professionals, both those who are and are not parents, and for parents who find that the average professional seldom sees their children and their problems from their point of view. It is more. It is a candid representation of the supreme frustration for a competent adult—a persistent problem which defies solution. Further, the problem is particularly difficult for persons oriented toward intellectual rather than emotional solutions to problems.

The problem confronted is the presence of a handicapped child or adult in the family of the professional. The reactions discussed are personal. The people are real; and the difficulties of the family seeking to cope with the crises of handicap, the insensitivities of the community, and the pain of societal ignorance are laid out in a way never before encountered in fifty years of literature on the subject.

Ann and Rud Turnbull, themselves parents-professionals, have tapped a new wellspring of insight into the problems of families with disabled children. While the professional is made to appear human, another message also comes through—you can be bright, competent, and successful but just as frustrated as the rest when your parental responsibilities and credentials are challenged.

This book does a great service. It allows professionals to speak to other professionals about some difficulties and challenges that most professionals have only heard from "nonprofessionals"—parents. It also addresses with force the continued dilemma of services for handicapped persons. Of all the people in a community, the professional should know how to get services. Yet, a frequent theme of the parents-professionals in this volume is failure to locate the health, educational, or social service required to meet the needs of their family in time of trial.

Finally, many parents have spoken about the strengthening aspect of working and living with handicapped children. Until now, few professionals have certified to that fact. The theme comes through time and again. Perhaps we will yet come to believe it. There is yet hope.

> Donald J. Stedman
> The University of North Carolina
> at Chapel Hill

Contents

Parents
Speak
Out

Burton Blatt

Burton Blatt, former president of the American Association on Mental Deficiency, is now the dean of the School of Education, Syracuse University, Syracuse, New York.

Introduction:
The Threatened Planet

The temptation is to write about the history of parent movements, about National Association for Retarded Citizens, United Cerebral Palsy, Association for Children with Learning Disabilities, and all the other organizations. The desire is to write about the authors of these chapters, about Gunnar Dybwad, Elizabeth Boggs, Allen Roeher, Jerry Weingold, Henry Cobb, about the many heroes who work towards the welfare of handicapped children, as well as one's anonymous opponents, which could be invigorating. Some temptations are foolish or cruel, and that's probably why many of those fulfilled are regretted. Because I think my histories and biographies will not help much and because I've already given my side about what happened and to whom, I'll try to resist the temptation this time. Then what is there to write about if not the history or the leaders? There are the unspeakable disagreements and the unexpressed gratitude and feeling. I'm going to try to explain in a roundabout way why parents and professionals have not been partners, why there are so few partners anywhere, and why we must work not only to rescue the handicapped but to save the planet.

Like the author of one of the chapters, Elsie Helsel, I, too, write letters. One is to parents of handicapped children, one to professionals, and the third to those who would read it. But, of course, feel free to read them all. That will please me.

Dear Parents:

There is little time for such things and really no need to pity a parent of a handicapped child. We should pity instead the person who does not try to understand how you must cope with otherwise ordinary affairs in extraordinary ways, how strong you have to be, and how much faith you must have to live beyond merely enduring. There are many of us who deserve such pity, though there should be so few.

Why don't people understand? I think because so many of us have the idea that we are special beyond comparison, unique beyond classification. Yet, who doesn't know that there are almost four billion people in the world and that, fundamentally, one is pretty much like another? Everyone knows that, but who remembers it? Most of us live our lives believing that everything about us is unique, that each of our discoveries remains undiscovered elsewhere, that our illnesses are not the illnesses that other people have, that our pain and sorrow and our pleasure and happiness are too deep to try to explain even to those closest to us. This strange belief in our uniqueness is surely what helps make the human being so different from other beings. Of course, this wonderful belief in our uniqueness is surely what makes us hard and unfeeling, and at times terrifying. Our uniqueness makes living fresh and wondrous. It also permits us to say cruel things in the name of science, religion, or parenthood.

We should remember that, in the end, even science won't help us out of the fix we got ourselves into. We must help each other. We should remember that for every wonder that science delivers, there is a price to be paid. For example, we are so good at using energy that we pollute almost everywhere energy is used. We are so good at keeping ourselves smelling good that mothers' milk now passes cancer to their babies. We are so good at traveling somewhere quickly that we have become rootless and our families are no longer families. Remember, in the end we are all we have. Remember, science is the solution to some problems but also the cause of others and, in fact, even the cause of those which it may eventually solve. People, too, are the cause and the solution.

You are now parents, but go back to your childhoods. While you were in school, it seemed all right that your teachers told small fibs when the truth might have made things awkward. It seemed all right to teach you that one river was like another river and that one person was like all other people. Although it may have seemed permissible to cut corners with the truth, those games are no longer permissible. Adults must tell the truth, especially to themselves. It's strange to see healthy and happy people out for the morning sun, riding bicycles on the avenue, without a seeming care in the world. How do they do it? How can they smile to themselves or laugh to each other, knowing what they know? How can a man drive to work each morning, whistling, so content that when he stops for a red light he removes a speck of lint from his camel-hair coat? It doesn't seem natural, people content, so glad with the state of things, as if nothing will change, as if a thing done is done forever. Isn't there someone around to blow the whistle on this mess, to say, "Look here, you're going to die. Forget that speck of dust. Go to church. Quit your current life. Do something. Try to find out what it's all about. Admit that the jig's up, that maybe there never was a jig"?

When the people discovered the Emperor really didn't have any clothes, they were satisfied. Their anxiety was relieved, their senses vindicated. And they were vexed with the Emperor for having subjected them to the embarrassing trick. Would they have been more compassionate if they had continued to look around and found that *they* didn't have any clothes either? Had they reached for that speck of lint a little less complacently, a little less automatically and absent mindedly, they might have realized there was no camel-hair coat, just the naked ape. Maybe that's why they were so easily taken in by the Emperor's hoax, because it was their own hoax. Maybe that's why they were so vexed with him, because they expected of emperors more than the everyday mortal hoax.

Everybody pretends with you, but you know that you're going to tell a lot of lies during your lifetime to yourself and to others. To illustrate the lies with which we live, I want to discuss the biggest lie, the denial of one's mortality.

We should examine the man whistling to work in his new Volvo. What's running through his head, in tune with the whistle and the sound of tires on pavement? Could these be his thoughts: Was the purchase of the radials a good deal? His wife? She's too radial. His job? It's too boring. How can he get more money? Or better radials? Those are the big problems he's thinking about.

Why is it that dying is one of the two most difficult ideas to think about, or to talk about? Because it is the most difficult idea to remember. We keep forgetting it's going to happen to each of us. We can't believe it, and that, too, is the problem. Dying is unbelievable. That's why living is the other most difficult idea to think about. Living, too, is unbelievable.

What can be done? Not much, except to stop the hand wringing, and to face facts. What are the facts? There aren't any. The one most fearful, most hopeful question people have—the question which only humans can ask, which in itself by its asking separates a human from other animals—is not answerable, nor can it ever be answerable by humans. Therefore, face life. The point is, one will never truly comprehend life's mysterious puzzles, but one should so arrange his life that he spends time struggling to understand the mysterious, even that which will never be understood. It isn't enough for a human being to escape the unknown or the difficult, to crowd the important questions and ideas out of his mind with questions of new tires or the widths of old ties. One shouldn't purge his system of that which a human being must face up to. One risks his life not when he faces hard problems, but when he denies seeking to understand the puzzle of his existence.

Dear Professionals:

There have hardly ever been partnerships between parents and professionals, and although the professionals are not entirely at fault, you know as well as I do that we could have done more to make those relationships better. Who can say why we didn't try harder to make it work? Maybe we didn't care enough, or we were too busy, or we didn't know how. Maybe, but those weren't main reasons. I think that close to main reasons is the idea we have that professionals and parents are too different to develop genuine collaborations, that we know so much and they know so little, that we are ever so much better. I think that many professionals have the idea that we can't possibly have the clients' nasty problems. The disease of professionals is that we believe we are too good for the illnesses and problems with which we are required to deal. The disease of consumers is that they believe us, that they refuse to remember that people are people, that all are in need of something and someone. When we became professionals, we forgot the golden rule; and consumers don't want to be reminded that if it should apply to them, it should apply to us.

How can we do better? One way is to seek criticism. Criticism binds professionals. It keeps facts together. It keeps ideas straight. It keeps movements in line. It's the glue and the gum. Criticism gums up innovation, gums up heterodoxy, gums up that which seems to be different. It tends to draw people and ideas toward the median. It protects the strong and can be fatal to the new and to the young. It causes strings to be played out, even when the game has ended. Criticism can be dangerous to intellectual health and human welfare because it can be a form of intrusion without guidance, license without the necessary responsibility, action without precision. Criticism is always defective because nothing worth criticizing is completely comprehensible. And it's a mirage, at once glue and glop; and a mirror, at once right and left; and a photographic image, at once positive and negative. It's as vital to the thinker as all of his references and notes. But it can be as silly as the radio preacher announcing, "The world ends today! But first, this message."

That's what it is. What it does is determined by who you are. Some people live by criticism. Others live off it. Most merely endure it. Know what it is and what it can do for you and to you. Although you may not make it your way of life—or your way to live—you may wish to do more than suffer with it. You can turn criticism to your purpose. It can become your touchstone rather than an intrusion that leaves worthless residue.

To make criticism work for you, know its elements. At the core is honest judgment, without which criticism cannot be useful to the recipient. Honesty permits criticism to be more evaluation than gossip, more out of colleagueship than maliciousness. Yet, telling the truth isn't nearly sufficient. It's rare enough but not enough. The truth alone hurts if it is not offered to help someone. Let me tell a story:

Once upon a time there was a small town king whose 25,000 subjects were all he had, and there were no others around in his kingdom to tell him the truth. Therefore, the king was the truth. By and by, a stranger came to the country. He knocked on the castle door, asking to see the king, and was shown in. It was an unlucky day for both of them. The stranger told the king the truth. The king had the stranger killed. Another ending to the story could have had the king kill himself. It can happen either way, so watch it.

Perhaps you will worry, "Can the truth kill me?"

It could. The truth is sure to kill you if you're the king and you think you have it. It's only pretty sure to kill you if you think others think you have it, so watch out for it if you believe you are a king. Watch out even if you don't believe you are. Truth is dangerous.

Criticism is truth's child. It, too, can kill. It, too, is the poison or the antidote. It generally is poisonous to kings and an antidote against becoming one, if taken in time.

But what about the more ordinary life, away from real kings and castles? What about one's life beyond criticism, beyond tomorrow? What about professionals as kings, and therefore as unique beings, as people immune to lay criticism? What about the king-professional who doesn't know yet must pretend to have the truth? When is uniqueness important? Variety is the spice of life. It's everywhere. Uniqueness, too, is the spice of life but by definition must remain a rarity. It's puzzling yet nevertheless true that variance does not lead to uniqueness. For example, everyone varies from everyone else in significant ways, yet as human beings no one is unique. Puzzling as it may be, to be different and yet a part of the human family remains one of life's anomalies. And for that reason alone, "When does the difference make a difference?" is an important question. Consider the schools. In usual ways, schools vary greatly. But how many schools are unique? Schools without walls vary greatly from walls with little schooling within, but each is not uncommon. Few schools are truly unique, not only because by definition uniqueness denotes rarity, but because uniqueness also refers to special qualities. For example, the king is more naked when his fly is open than when his glove is lost. There are degrees of uniqueness as there are degrees of nakedness, such as stark nakedness, like a nude king, and the trivial, as when he loses his glove. It's always trivial when dealing with a lost glove. Running around with one's pants down in a clothed society is always unique.

We should have rules about the relationships between rules and exceptions. One might be that we don't endorse the exceptions as the rule.

Another might be that we don't support a law that discourages exceptions and that we don't support a practice that would convert unique situations to regular occurrences. If we did, it would be the beginning of the end. Here's why.

A murderer can be apprehended and dealt with, but what can be done when the law itself promotes the exception, the murder? When exceptions are kept as exceptions, murder can be contained. We know who the bad guy is and who should get it. But who gets it when government itself is corrupt, when the crime is the rule? Take Spandau. Take the hundreds of guards, officials, and politicians watching Rudolph Hess, and each other. Take Willowbrook Developmental Center. At various times, the courts have ordered repatriation of its residents. Now, what should we make of a place where the goal is to evacuate? "Let's get these poor bastards out of here. They've had enough." Should we think well of a place that holds out repatriation as reward? Yale doesn't cluck its institutional tongue with glee when one of its students transfers to MIT or the community college. Well, that's how the Willowbrook fellows seem to have it figured out. It seems that mental health's one claim to sanity and decency is that they are finding placements for their clients outside of the terrible institutions they run. It seems that as long as a few inmates are kept around the asylum to justify the jobs and resources, all of the others could be sent to better rewards. But the options which may have once made an interesting patchwork quilt may now be bogus cloth, raggedy and useless.

Variety is not a virtue; it's given. Uniqueness is what connects with quality. Changing the rules, or making the exception the rule and the rule the exception, may not enhance quality. Variety is indeed a spice of life. So is uniqueness. But the quality of the main course is what matters most in the meal.

I had a terrible vision this morning. Terrible morning visions are the worst ones, worse than nightmares. This scene had me in control of one of the magic time-frozen cameras that weathermen use to show the full day's sky in a few instants. My camera was pointed at the state asylum day after day, year after year. I saw the traditional institutionalization policy at work, leading to the inevitable inhuman treatments. I then saw the vigorous reforms, so vigorous that revolution whispered, sedition beckoned, so much so that there was actual change. The institution began to emit from its bowels the refuse of uncomfortable constipations. But I also saw the strategies of those in charge. "Take who should go. Take those whose time had come. But leave us our hard core and ourselves. Leave us be. Let us live." I saw the institution nearly emptied of all except a few who needed to remain or else the institution itself would have to die and, thus, the caretakers would have to die.

What do the world's stewards say, the caretakers? Yes, empty Spandau, but you must leave our Hess be. Without Hess, we are nothing. Without the poor, there are no rich. Without the sick, there are no healthy. Without the bad, there is no good. Everything exists by comparison, by counterpoint. Everything has a positive and a negative, a template and an outline, a pressure and a mark, an outside and a center. And some things must be preserved if for nothing else but to serve as comparison objects. Some people must be in certain places, so other people may be there, too. Our dependency on one another is a bond that is stronger than fears and strengths. Hess will never be free. But neither shall we. There is justice. We are the proof.

Yes, everything is a circle. For everything there's a pull. For everything there's a center. But know your circles. You have free wills. Strive to comprehend the pulls and the reasons. You must find your center. Without a center, a human being is a mannequin, an image without a life, tone without meaning. You must search for the core of your circle. In the center of your circle are your answers. Don't believe the caretakers.

Dear Someone:

It's awful what we have done to each other. It's awful what we have done to the planet. We are racing willfully to the end. This is almost the last straw. Now we have polluted mother's milk. Yes, we must solve the puzzles of retardation and what it does to individuals and families, but the beginning analysis to such puzzles is not to be found in the child's condition but in the planet's condition. The final judgment will not sentence the child but the planet. Deal with your child's illness, dose him, and love him. The only treatment that fully satisfies anyone is found not when we tamper with the body but when we touch the soul, and thus each other. The planet is threatened, not because of what we don't know about but because of what we don't care about. While illnesses are man's curse, handicaps (stigmas attached to illness) are his invention, and we have yet to learn the difference. While we still have a lot to learn about illnesses, we have everything to learn about handicaps. You must understand that, even though not all illnesses have effective treatments, all handicaps are preventable and curable. Handicaps are conditions of the soul.

Why are there more and more lifeless scenes freezing before you? Or is it about only me that I write? I don't think so, but I want to check this out with you. Why is it that there are more and more bodies around, people dressed for a party when there is no party? Why does it seem that we are in states of perpetual readiness, waiting to begin the fun, the race, the job, the love, but always only waiting. There is nothing to do and nowhere to go and nobody to be with. There seems to be too many fast planes and cars to take us to wait, or to nowhere, or to bring us to and from nobody. There's so much doing for so little to do and for so little being done. Do you too feel that way? You may not feel that way if you do not know about the old days. There was once a time when everything and everybody was alive. You could see life and hear it. Best of all, you could smell it. More than anything else, life has certain unmistakable smells. The people. The air. The homes. Of course, food. The schools. Weren't the old-school smells wonderful reassurances? Not only the school paste but even the books themselves. The smells told us that mathematics was coming up, there was always a lunchtime, and there was always something big to look forward to, like assembly or the annual visit to the Museum of Natural History. All such news was to be read in the smells. And is losing one's keenness of smell what getting old is supposed to be? But eyes can't ever be fooled. One's eyes won't fool him, if he doesn't want to be fooled. The paint and neon doesn't hide the tawdriness of Times Square. The grime can't camouflage the grandeur of those lions sitting guard at the Fifth Avenue Library. Nobody is ever fooled more than he wants to be. Good is good. And there are good and not-so-good societies.

I don't anymore hear a person wish that he could leave this world a better place than he found it. I wonder it it's because most of us have given up the ghost of such dreams. Or is it because most of us are too obsessed with material gain, the acquisition of power, having fun and thrills to bother with tidying up the planet? Whatever the reasons, doing something special for this world seems to be an old-fashioned idea. Nevertheless, it also seems to be an important idea. For somebody who wants more from life than wealth, power, or even continuous fun and excitement, it still seems to be a very good idea.

One reason why wanting to leave this world a better place may be a good idea is because no one will take you seriously for having it. It's like academic freedom. "So what?" some will say. Hardly anyone realizes that those who want to leave the world a better place are among the most powerful people on earth. But those people don't always appreciate that the reason they are so powerful is because they are viewed as harmless, the strength which most people believe is their weakness. Indeed, if there were not such a perception, do-gooders would be exiled or worse. But they are not exiled, they are free to do good. You can be free to improve this planet, and I think you may succeed if you begin in a small way.

One of the serious diseases of our times is the belief that bigger is better. We have a penchant to find room for everything. While Thoreau insisted that a human being can do without this luxury or that triviality, we insist that everything is a necessity and nothing a luxury. The burden is on us to reject useless electric can openers that make people less useful and gold toothpicks that make people sillier. The disease has several symptoms. It causes one to want to do more rather than to do better. Like obese people, we seem sure that among the calories that please our palates are the calories that nourish our cells. And like the obese, we don't want to know the consequences. We don't want to know what all the useless bigness and puffery does to people.

The prescription: All things being equal, smaller is better. Think about a small brimming cup rather than a huge almost-empty caldron. Think about the meaning of the biblical prayer of gratitude for one's cup that runs over. And don't be alarmed. A refrigerator may be smaller, but it will contain enough to keep us healthy. Unnecessary consumption is a disease, only sometimes of the body but always of the spirit.

Unnecessary consumption denies the idea that everything must count or nothing counts. Every person must have a place, must be here for a special reason, or no one has a place, or no one has a special reason for being. Either everybody counts or nobody counts.

Unnecessary consumption denies the connection between our lives and the course of world history. It not only denies our responsibility to try to see the connection but it denies our responsibility to take part actively in the history making.

I am not concerned only with the energy crisis, although one is obviously worried about that bit of bad news. I am concerned about how we abuse nature and use science. We are like children who learn to use crayons, insisting on using them all over the floors and windows. Certainly, it's a joy to exercise a newly mastered skill or machine. But we have used the crayon of science all over, too—over our homes and over our children and our minds and maybe over our souls. For those of us with the crayons, it was good fun. But we got carried away. Now we will have to clean up the mess and see if we can use this thing "science" in a more grown-up way.

What I have tried to say is that the world we have can be a good one once we realize what it is we need rather than want. What we need will have something to do with lowered thermostats and car pools and hand-operated can openers. Of course, it will have something to do with our compromises concerning everything mysterious. What I have tried to say is that to save the planet we must first save ourselves, then each other. And to save ourselves we must save the planet. Everything is related. Everybody is dependent.

Philip Roos

Philip Roos is executive director of the National Association for Retarded Children (name changed to National Association for Retarded Citizens in October 1973), appointed to the job on January 1, 1969.

He was the associate commissioner in the New York State Department of Mental Hygiene, Division of Mental Retardation, from December 1967 until he assumed his present position.

He was superintendent of the Austin State School, Austin, Texas, from 1963 to 1967, and served as director of Psychological Services with the Texas Department of Mental Health and Mental Retardation from 1960 to 1963. While serving as superintendent, he also functioned for one year as the director of Community Mental Retardation Services for the state of Texas.

He lives in Arlington, Texas, and has a fifteen-year-old retarded daughter who resides at Denton State School in Texas.

Parents of Mentally Retarded Children – Misunderstood and Mistreated

I was fortunate in having established myself as a professional in the field of mental retardation before I became a parent of a retarded child. I was knowledgeable about mental retardation, as well as mental health, and knew how professionals operated. I could even converse with them in their professional jargons and interpret their cryptic statements. Furthermore, I had achieved some professional status, knew many professionals as colleagues, and had at least some insight into my own reactions to having a retarded child. I should have found it easy to obtain competent professional assistance, and things should have gone as smoothly as humanly possible.

Things did not go smoothly, though. Surprisingly, my wife and I embarked on a long series of catastrophic interactions with professionals which echoed the complaints I had heard so often from other parents. As a result of these experiences, I refined my earlier concepts of professional mishandling of parents of retarded children as well as my interpretation of parental reactions to having a retarded child.

Professional Goofs

In a previous marriage, my wife had given birth to a profoundly retarded daughter and had had a series of spontaneous abortions. I solicited opinions from geneticists as to the likelihood of her giving birth to another retarded child. My wife and I were reassured that the danger was negligible. Nonetheless, we selected a pediatrician who seemed particularly sensitive to problems of mental retardation: his wife was a neurologist. I spoke to him prior to the birth of our daughter Val about my wife's history and our concern regarding the new baby. I asked him to be particularly alert to the possibility of mental retardation.

Val's early months were characterized by colic, hyperactivity, inattentiveness, total absence of social response, and sleep disturbances. During the latter part of her first year, she became increasingly hyperactive, would spend hours banging her head against her crib, and failed to reach the typical landmarks in sensorimotor development. As I repeatedly pointed out these indications of developmental anomolies to our pediatrician, he would gaze at my wife and me with obvious disbelief and assure us that the baby was quite normal; we were anxious parents. This and subsequent episodes led me to formulate the concept of *professional ignorance:* the unfortunate fact that many professionals simply do not know about mental retardation and have failed to recognize it or misdiagnose it and, all too often, give parents misinformation or fallacious advice.

At fourteen months, our daughter could not stand alone, did not talk, seemed to understand nothing, and did not seem to recognize my wife and me. Our pediatrician decided the problem stemmed from her feet; we were referred to any orthopedist who prescribed a complex brace which the child wore at night and part of each day to correct the alignment of her feet. We had embarked on what I labelled "referral ad infinitum" or the "hot potato game": the tendency of some professionals to refer hapless parents from specialist to specialist. This tendency may, of course, reflect a genuine search for answers to complex situations, yet I became convinced that it was sometimes less the result of professional ignorance than the professional's reluctance to confront parents with the reality of their child's retardation. In some cases it seems that professionals are less able to accept retardation in a child than the child's own parents.

Clinging stubbornly to the conclusion that our daughter was "probably just fine," our pediatrician next referred us to a neurologist. Since this worthy was a consultant to the large state institution for the retarded of which I was the superintendent, I felt confident that he would immediately recognize the obvious signs of severe retardation in our child. Imagine my consternation when, after failing to accomplish even a funduscopic (vision) examination on Val due to her extreme hyperactivity, the learned consultant cast a baleful eye on my wife and me and informed us that the child was quite normal. On the other hand, he continued, her parents were obviously neurotically anxious, and he would prescribe tranquilizers for us. I had suddenly been demoted from the role of a professional to that of "the parent as patient": the assumption by some professionals that parents of a retarded child are emotionally maladjusted and are prime candidates for counseling, psychotherapy, or tranquilizers. My attempts to point out the many indications of developmental delays and neurological disturbances were categorically dismissed as manifestations of my "emotional problems." I was witnessing another captivating professional reaction—the "deaf ear syndrome": the attitude on the part of some professionals that parents are complete ignoramuses so that any conclusion they reach regarding their own child is categorically ignored. Later I found that suggestions I would make regarding my own child would be totally dismissed by some professionals, while these same suggestions made as a professional about other children would be cherished by my colleagues as professional pearls of wisdom. Parenthetically, when I wrote to the neurologist years later to inform him that Val's condition had been clearly diagnosed as severe mental retardation and that she had been institutionalized, he did not reply.

This interchange also illustrated another problem faced by parents; namely, *professional omniscience* and *omnipotence:* the myth that professionals possess the source of all ultimate knowledge and can make wise decisions affecting other people's destinies. This unfortunate myth has been frequently perpetrated by professionals as well as by parents.

At last our pediatrician reluctantly agreed with me when I once again confronted him with the overwhelming evidence that Val was mentally retarded. Yet he clung to the possibility that rather than mental retardation the problem might be less "hopeless," perhaps autism or childhood schizophrenia. This attitude of *professional hopelessness* toward mental retardation as an "incurable disease" is still rather prevalent among those who operate within a medical model. Unfortunately, it generates self-fulfilling and self-limiting prophesies which impede the development of retarded individuals. Furthermore, parents easily detect such defeatist attitudes and either develop similar expectations or resent those who adopt such a negative approach toward their child.

To clarify his diagnosis of Val, our pediatrician next sent us to a child psychiatrist (also one of my consultants at the state institution) with a strong psychoanalytic orientation. This very conscientious practitioner attacked the challenge with obvious interest and dedication. He began with the traditional multidisciplinary team evaluation, wherein my wife reiterated one more time her many painful past experiences. We were to go through this traumatic recounting of past agonies many times over, as if each new professional began with a tabula rasa rather than with a thick file in which all the gruesome details of the history were already minutely compiled. I eventually hypothesized that some professionals must suffer either from a compulsion to uncover other people's personal past or from a pervasive distrust of their colleagues, leading to the need to repeat other's work.

One day the child psychiatrist proudly announced to my wife and me that the evaluation was complete and that he would discuss it with us. I was much gratified to find that he did not try to hide behind the veil of secrecy which, at that time, was so prevalent among professionals. It seemed that many professionals were reluctant to share information with their clients, allegedly because it might be too threatening, too uncomfortable, or in some other way destructive to the client. Our psychiatrist, on the other hand, bravely read parts of the report to us, including our daughter's IQ and the conclusion that Val's problem was unknown, although autism or childhood schizophrenia seemed to be plausible alternatives. Since I was surprised by the relatively high IQ which seemed markedly incongruent with Val's behavior, I asked for the mental age. As I had feared, the mental age was very low, and it was obvious that the psychologist had made a computational error in calculating the IQ. When I remarked on this to the psychiatrist, who knew I had been a practicing clinical psychologist, he ventured that my own emotional needs might be preventing me from accepting his psychologist's findings and encouraged me to explore this avenue (the "parent as patient" role again). At my insistence, he subsequently asked his psychologist to review his findings and reported back that, indeed, the IQ had been erroneously determined and that rather than falling in the dull normal range, it fell in the area of severe mental retardation. Had I not been a trained psychologist, my wife and I (and the psychiatrist) would have proceeded on the erroneous assumption that Val was really of dull normal intelligence and therefore that her grossly primitive behavior must be the result of some cause other than mental retardation.

Indeed, our child psychiatrist did not accept the diagnosis of severe mental retardation. He undertook weekly joint sessions with

Val, my wife, and me to determine the cause of the problem and to counsel with us. In spite of my intimate familiarity with psychotherapy and psychoanalytic theory, I could not help but marvel at some of the ingenious and imaginative interpretations and recommendations arising from these weekly sessions.

On one occasion, for example, the psychiatrist accused me of withholding critical information when in the course of a discussion I casually mentioned a pet monkey who had been in our home during Val's earliest months. In an attempt to interject a bit of desperately needed humor into the situation, I replied, with tongue in cheek, that I must have repressed my memory of the monkey due to my feelings of guilt for having given the animal away. To my horror the psychiatrist took this as his cue for a lengthy discourse on the dynamics of repression and guilt, which was followed by the imaginative interpretation that Val's problem could stem from intense sibling rivalry with the unfortunate monkey. He insisted we purchase a toy facsimile of the departed beast and place it in her crib, so her reaction to it could be observed. Alas, her reaction was no different from her reaction to anything else placed in the crib—the toy was summarily tossed on the floor without the slightest hint that she recognized it as a symbol from the past.

On another occasion we were startled to hear the psychiatrist describe the use of Chihuahuas in Mexico as foot warmers placed in beds on cold winter nights. My wife and I exchanged anxious glances, fearing for the good doctor's sanity. The relevance of his dramatic account of Mexican foot warmers became evident, however, when he prescribed one Chihuahua in Val's crib every night as a source of unconditional nurture; he generously offered his own dog on a loan basis. Rather than reacting defensively to the doctor's implicit message that his ignorant dog could supply Val what he felt her parents could not, I asked a practical question—was the dog housebroken? No, it was not. And so it went.

It would be counterproductive to continue with personal examples of professional mishandling. Most parents of retarded children can easily top anything which I experienced since, as I stated earlier, I was fortunate in being a professional in the field of mental retardation.

I do not mean to imply that all professionals mishandle parents, nor even that those described did nothing right. On the contrary, they were sometimes helpful and almost always had good intentions. Their mishandling was the result of ignorance and improper training rather than maliciousness or indifference. No doubt things have improved in recent years (my experience occurred in the early 1960s), yet similar reports from parents are still common today, and training in mental retardation is still woefully lacking in the curriculum for many professional degrees, including medicine.

In all fairness, it must be recognized that professionals may also be mishandled by parents. Indeed, a sort of vicious cycle may develop as professional mishandling generates frustration in parents who retaliate by mishandling professionals. Likewise, parental mishandling of professionals tends to reinforce professionals' negative stereotypes of parents which fosters the mishandling of parents.

Parental Reactions

When I found that I had become the parent of a retarded child, I was no stranger to the emotional reactions which I experienced. As a matter of fact, I had written and lectured on the subject (Roos, 1963). Although similar emotional reactions and conflicts are probably common to most parents, their handling of the situation varies considerably. While some may be totally overwhelmed by having a retarded child, others cope constructively and grow as a result of their experience. It would be a serious mistake to assume that most parents of retarded children are emotionally disturbed.

In a society such as ours which greatly values intelligence, mental retardation is a formidable handicap. The tendency to equate humanness with intelligence is common (e.g., Fletcher, 1972), and the perception of retarded persons as subhuman organisms is still prevalent (Wolfensberger, 1969). Hence most parents—though well adjusted—faced with having a retarded child are likely to experience major psychological stress. The most common patterns which I had identified as the result of clinical experience, understanding of personality dynamics, and work with parents of retarded children include the following (Roos, 1963):

1. *Loss of Self-Esteem.* Because of our tendency to experience our children as extensions of ourselves, a defective child is likely to threaten our self-esteem. We may question our own worth and abandon some of our long-range goals when it becomes obvious that our child will be unable to achieve as we had hoped.

2. *Shame.* While most parents take pride in their children's accomplishments, parents of a retarded child learn to anticipate social rejection, pity, or ridicule. Their love of their handicapped child is only a partial protection against the feelings of shame generated when their

child is pointed out as a deviant or when other children laugh at him. Even after many years of such exposure, I am still not completely immune to the furtive whispers between parents and children which greet my retarded daughter when she ventures on a playground or into a store with me.

3. *Ambivalence*. The mixed feelings of love and anger typically experienced by parents toward their children are usually greatly intensified toward a retarded child. The greater the frustration generated by the retarded child's irritating behavior and failure to learn, the more likely are the parents to feel anger and resentment. Fantasies of the child's death are not uncommon. Since these feelings are typically accompanied by guilt, some parents may react with overprotection while others tend to reject their child.

4. *Depression*. Most parents are deeply disappointed in having a retarded child and realistically concerned with his future. To some, mental retardation symbolizes the death of the child and may lead to the type of grief reaction associated with the loss of a loved one. In any case, chronic sorrow can be anticipated as a nonpathological reaction to having a retarded child (Olshansky, 1966).

5. *Self-Sacrifice*. Some parents seem to dedicate themselves totally to their retarded child, make great personal sacrifices, and adopt a martyr approach to life. Sometimes this pattern leads to family disruption, including neglect of other children and marital conflicts.

6. *Defensiveness*. Professionals are familiar with parents who have become hypersensitive to perceived criticism of their retarded child. Often these parents respond to inferred criticism with resentment and belligerence. In extreme cases, parents may deny that their child is retarded, rationalize his shortcomings, and seek professional opinions to substantiate their own conviction that there is really nothing wrong with him.

As my wife and I struggled with our feelings regarding Val's mental retardation, we became aware that, although we certainly experienced some of the feelings just described, we were more preoccupied by the reactivation of old conflicts and anxieties. These conflicts and anxieties were not specific to having a retarded child; rather, they seemed inherent in the human condition as experienced by most people, and that having a retarded child merely tends to exacerbate them. Yet, I have not heard them discussed by either professionals or parents. My wife and I found that professionals seemed strangely disinclined to listen to our concerns, and I still find these fundamental existential conflicts seem to be completely neglected by professionals in the field of mental retardation. I suspect that many professionals may feel uncomfortable discussing such conflicts, probably because they are common to most members of our society and usually lie relatively dormant in most people. Professionals apparently prefer to deal with the traditional "parental pathology" and effectively avoid recognizing parents' existential conflicts. They may have no simple answers to these conflicts and may become anxious because of the potential reactivation of their own unresolved conflicts.

The most critical conflict areas which are likely to be reactivated by the realization of having a retarded child include the following:

1. *Disillusionment.* As children we are taught to develop totally unrealistic expectations, such as success, achievement, wealth, love, and status. We expect wise parents, loving and lovable mates, and perfect children. Experience gradually erodes these unrealistic expectations of ourselves and others, leading to a long series of disillusionments in ourselves, in others, and in life in general.

Many of us channel our frustrated yearning for perfection into our children, through whom we hope to realize our thwarted dreams of accomplishment and happiness. Unfortunately, a retarded child is usually an unsuitable vehicle for fulfilling these hopes, so he represents a major disillusionment—often the culmination of a long series of disappointments. If the parents do not have other children, the possibility of them finding fulfillment through their children must be abandoned. Parents may then desperately search for other avenues to self-enhancement, or they may slip into pervasive feelings of hopelessness.

2. *Aloneness.* The need for intimacy seems to be universal, but no one can transcend his individual boundaries and fully share his feelings and perceptions with another. Often the last desperate hope of overcoming aloneness is through our children—products of our bodies, shaped into our image, literally extensions of ourselves. But a retarded child may not be able to fulfill this need because of limited capacity to communicate and to achieve intimacy. The parents of such a child may feel that they have lost their final chance to achieve intimacy and may become overwhelmed with feelings of aloneness.

3. *Vulnerability.* Most of us begin life with the fantasy that we are all-powerful. As we mature, we learn to recognize our own helpless-

ness and gradually recognize that others, too, are not omnipotent, including parents, teachers, and heroes. Pain, injury, illness, and failure repeatedly confront us with our personal vulnerability, the tenuousness of our control over the world, and, indeed, the fragile nature of life itself. Mental retardation in one's child reactivates these feelings of vulnerability. We are painfully reminded that our most precious possessions, our dearest dreams, can be completely destroyed and that we are totally helpless to do anything about it.

4. Inequity. Our nation is founded on the principle of justice for all, and we are taught from earliest childhood that fairness and justice ultimately prevail. "Good" will triumph, and if our judicial system falters, some greater force will reward heroes and punish villains. When faced with retardation in his child, a parent may feel overwhelmed with the enormity of the apparent inequity, and his natural reaction is to ask, "Why me?" In trying to answer this question, he may conclude either that he deserves the punishment because of grievous sins or that the world is neither fair nor just. The former alternative leads to guilt, remorse, and self-recrimination; the latter threatens basic ethical, moral, and religious beliefs.

5. Insignificance. Young children typically imagine that they are important figures occupying a central role in the scheme of things. Maturity brings with it the realization of personal insignificance, yet most of us are raised to yearn for greatness or, at least, meaning. When greatness escapes us, we search for meaning in filling satisfying social roles, such as those of husband, wife, father, mother, and so forth. When we are frustrated in achieving a rewarding parental role—as can easily occur with a retarded child—we are vulnerable to feelings of insignificance by being deprived of an important opportunity to achieve meaning.

6. Past Orientation. Most parents anticipate their children's future with enthusiasm, expecting such happy events as scholastic achievement, success in sports, graduation, marriage, birth of grandchildren, and promising careers. In contrast, parents of a retarded child usually view their child's future with apprehension, anticipating scholastic failure, exclusion from services (educational, social, recreational), inability to work or menial employment, problems in sexual adjustment, inability to live independently, and a life of loneliness and isolation. Realistically, services tend to become less adequate as the retarded person ages, increasing the parents' frustrations. Hence, while most normal people are future oriented, parents of a retarded child tend to retreat from the future as a source of pain and shift toward past orientation and from an optimistic to a pessimistic attitude toward what lies ahead.

7. *Loss of Immortality*. The anticipation of our own inevitable death is, for many of us, a major source of existential anxiety. One common approach to coping with this anxiety is to seek symbolic immortality through one's children. Grandparents' legendary delight with their grandchildren illustrates our emphasis on continuation of the family line. When a child is retarded, however, this potential avenue to immortality is threatened; when the child is an only child, this chance for immortality is denied the parents, and they are faced with their finiteness and ultimate loss of identity.

Parents and Professionals Working Together

During recent years parents of retarded children and professionals have been drawing closer together. They often work effectively as members of multidisciplinary teams as well as advocates for retarded persons. Nonetheless, their interactions are still often marred by friction and sometimes overt conflict. The very complexity of working with a retarded individual and the resulting frustrations are likely to generate tensions. The unfortunate fact that mental retardation is still "uncurable" and all too often imposes serious limits on individual development is a constant source of consternation to both professionals and parents. Furthermore, difficulties between parents and professionals can often stem from destructive stereotypes, from professional mishandling, or from unresolved parental emotional problems.

In addition to these common sources of difficulties, other types of issues are often unrecognized and can become troublesome. I have found that the following types of issues need to be clearly recognized and openly discussed if parents and professionals are to avoid working at cross-purposes.

1. *Values*. All to frequently, professionals and parents assume that they hold the same values regarding what is desirable for the retarded individual. Yet, the values held by the parents and the professionals may be incompatible, leading to conflicts regarding program objectives and long-range goals.

For example, the assumption by parents and professionals both is usually made that services for the mentally retarded are devoted to serve retarded clients. This assumption is not always valid, however, since other beneficiaries can include the retarded person's family (e.g., parental frustrations due to having a retarded child in the home can be reduced), the agency operating the service (e.g., increased budgets and expanded staffs can be justified), the professional in charge of the program (e.g., a favorable reputation can be established) and society (e.g., the number of "tax burdens" can be decreased). It is now well recognized that the needs of these various individuals are not always identical, and that in some instances, even the needs of parents and their child may be incompatible.

Even when the beneficiary of a service is clearly the mentally retarded client, there still may be confusion regarding the implicit values on which program objectives are based. Examples of currently popular values, which may at times lead to incompatible objectives, include the following:

Foster maximum individual development so that the client reaches his potential.

Provide the client with conditions which are as much as possible like conditions of normal persons.

Make each retarded person as happy as possible.

Help each client become as economically independent as possible.

Help each retarded person to act as much as possible like nonretarded persons.

Achieve the greatest possible level of emotional independence for each retarded individual.

2. *Objectives and Priorities.* Parents and professionals may have different ideas regarding specific program objectives and their relative importance. For example, professionals may focus on academic and abstract achievements whereas parents may be interested in practical objectives which make the retarded child easier to live with. Professionals may emphasize development of new skills, such as number concepts or color recognition, while parents may wish to eliminate socially inappropriate behavior, such as tantrums or screaming. As a result of these different priorities, professionals may feel a child is making good progress while his parents may feel that nothing is happening. I recall, for instance, that some years ago my wife and I were told with pride that Val was beginning to recognize colors. Rather than reacting with obvious enthusiasm, we expressed dismay that she had managed to yank all her hair from her head. We

suggested that eliminating this self-destructive behavior should take precedence over color recognition.

3. Temporal Orientation. As already noted, parents of retarded children may feel threatened by what they fear the future holds for them and their retarded children, so long-range goals may be avoided or rejected by parents. On the other hand, professionals may structure their programs in terms of such goals. For example, middle-class parents may reject the goal of their child working in a marginal service job, whereas the child's teacher may consider this to be a very desirable outcome. On the other hand, parents' emphasis on current irritations may appear trivial to professionals. To parents who must cope with daily problems of living, however, eliminating current frustrations may seem much more urgent than working toward distant goals, whose value they may seriously question.

4. Competition. It may seem ironic that parents and professionals may interact competitively, but I am convinced that feelings of competitiveness are often present, although neither parents nor professionals may be aware of them. Parents may feel hurt that a stranger is more successful than they are with their child, and professionals may feel threatened that untrained and unsophisticated parents may succeed where they have failed. As a result, parents and professionals may surreptitiously undermine and downgrade each other's efforts.

Based on my personal experience as both a parent and a professional, as well as observation of many parent-professional interactions, I submit the following suggestions for fostering productive work between parents and professionals:

1. Parents should be accepted as full-fledged members of the multidisciplinary team. They should be considered as colleagues, and their contributions should be treated with respect.
2. Parents and professionals should recognize that they may have preconceived notions about each other which may interfere with working together. Destructive stereotypes and negative expectations should be openly discussed whenever possible.
3. Professionals should try to accept parents "where they are" (in their attitude toward mental retardation) and develop the skill to listen and encourage full disclosure. Most effective counselors, I am convinced, have learned to develop good ears while restraining their tongue. Professionals should resist

the temptation to criticize parental attitudes so as not to stifle free expression of feelings or reinforce feeling of guilt and worthlessness. Before parents can develop constructive attitudes toward their handicapped child, they must come to grips with whatever negative feelings may exist.

4. Professionals should be particularly attuned to the existential anxieties experienced by parents of retarded children, and they must be willing to listen to expressions of these anxieties.

5. Professionals should share all relevant information that is the basis for planning and decision making with parents. Information should be furnished as soon as it becomes available to minimize parents' anxieties resulting from ambiguity and threat of the unknown. Unless there are compelling reasons to withhold specific information, parents should be furnished with the same data, including test findings and written reports, as other team members.

6. Clear two-way communication is essential to productive parent-professional interaction. Professional jargon should be avoided as much as possible and technical terms should be simply explained. Parents as well as professionals should indicate whenever they suspect that they are not completely clear as to what is being communicated.

7. In general, professionals should have the prime responsibility for selecting the methods and techniques to be used, and parents—or, when appropriate, the clients themselves—should be ultimately responsible for selecting goals and objectives. Whenever possible, these should be joint decisions involving parents, clients, and professionals. In reaching these decisions, parents and clients must be furnished all relevant information, including a description of available alternatives. If professional members of the team feel that a parental decision is not in the best interest of the retarded client, the matter should be referred to an independent committee charged with review of ethical and legal issues. The establishment, composition, and functions of such committees have been described in detail (e.g., AAMD, 1975; May et al., 1975; *Wyatt v. Stickney*, 1972), and they are now commonly assigned to programs and facilities serving retarded clients.

8. Parents as well as professionals need support and encouragement as they try to cope with the problems and frustrations of helping a retarded individual. Mutual reinforcement, praise, and encouragement can be very useful.

9. Parents and professionals should guard against competing against each other. They need to be constantly aware of the possibility of competitive rivalries and of the temptation to use each other as scapegoats or to undermine each other's efforts with the retarded client.

Conclusion

Over twenty-five years ago, parents of retarded children founded what is now the National Association for Retarded Citizens (NARC), largely as a reaction against professional neglect, rejection, and mishandling. In the ensuing years NARC has grown into a potent force on behalf of retarded persons. Gradually parents and friends of the retarded have been joined by professionals as effective social change agents, participating jointly in major legislative efforts and landmark litigation. Recently, parents and professionals have embarked on cooperative team efforts to educate and habilitate retarded persons. Mutual respect and understanding are growing as the old myths and destructive stereotypes are slowly fading away.

References

American Association on Mental Deficiency. *Position papers of the American Association on Mental Deficiency.* Washington: Author, 1975.

Fletcher, J. Indicators of humanhood: A tentative profile of man. In *The Hastings Center report* (Vol. 2, No. 5). Hastings-on-Hudson, New York: Hastings Center, 1972.

May, J.G., Risley, T.R., Twardosz, S., Friedman, P., Bijou, S., & Wexler, O. *Guidelines for the use of behavioral procedures in state programs for retarded persons.* Arlington, Tex.: National Association for Retarded Citizens, 1975.

National Association for Retarded Citizens. *Parent/professional Training Project Booklet III.* Arlington, Tex.: Author, in press.

Olshansky, S. Parent responses to a mentally defective child. *Mental Retardation*, 1966, *4*, 21–23.

Roos, P. Psychological counseling with parents of retarded children. *Mental Retardation*, 1963, *1*, 345–350.

Roos, P. Changing patterns of residential services. In *National Conference on Residential Care.* Arlington, Tex.: National Association for Retarded Citizens, 1969.

Roos, P. Parent organizations. In J. Wortis (Ed.), *Mental Retardation—An annual review* (Vol. 3). New York: Grune and Stratton, 1970.

Roos, P. Parents of mentally retarded persons. *International Journal of Mental Health,* 1977, 6(1), 96–119.

Wolfensberger, W. The origin and nature of our institutional models. In R.B. Kugel & W. Wolfensberger (Eds.), *Changing patterns of residential services for the mentally retarded.* Washington: The President's Committee on Mental Retardation, 1969.

Wyatt v. Stickney, 344 F. Supp. 373 (M. D. Ala., 1972).

Jane Schulz

Jane Schulz is an associate professor and coordinator of the Mental Retardation Program in the Department of Special Education at Western Carolina University. After serving on the university faculty for five years, she took a year off to serve as a resource teacher in the local public schools. For several summers, she has coordinated a one-month camping/educational program for severely retarded children. Jane has been a member of a human rights committee at a residential institution and has served as the president of the North Carolina Federation of the Council for Exceptional Children.

Jane's son, Billy, recently graduated from high school and is earning minimum wage as a worker in a lumber business.

The Parent –
Professional Conflict

Articles, books, and lectures dealing with the education of handicapped children seem to agree wholeheartedly on one point: the team approach is indicated. While the composition of the team may vary with the disability, the discipline, or the situation, usually the classroom teacher and the parents are prominent members. This is certainly appropriate, for who spends more time and energy with the handicapped child than the teacher and the parents? Who is more involved, more concerned, more knowledgeable?

When I was teaching kindergarten, a young mother approached me at registration and said, "I want Angie to be in your class because she needs help and I understand you have a handicapped child." This and similar experiences have indicated to me the strength of the parent-teacher combination. Couldn't the parent-teacher *team* function in the same role?

While there are probably many parents and teachers who work well together towards the best education for the child, traditionally there is a conflict. In describing the growth and functions of parent groups, Cain (1976) recently noted that parents, through negative experiences with educators, have lacked confidence in professionals. He stated that while attitudes are now more positive, the professional usually acts in an advisory capacity.

The parent of a hearing-impaired child has described the efforts required to establish and maintain a cooperative working relationship with the schools. She finds that it is not easy to ask for additional services, conferences, or evaluations. She feels it is essential to ask and to continue to ask if you care about your child's education (Kean, 1975).

My own experience supports these statements. As a parent, I am critical of the educational system which, I feel, has not served the needs of my child. As an educator I am, in part, responsible for the inefficiency of the system and therefore the object of my own dissatisfaction.

Why is such a logical, essential relationship literally inoperable? One of the factors cited by professionals most frequently is the attitude of the parents. As a parent, I am sensitive to this allegation; as a teacher, I know it is true. Parents appear to fall into two categories: the overprotective and the uncaring. Another observation I gained from my experience as a kindergarten teacher occurred when the children were separated from parents. The children sometimes cried; this seemed to please the parents who were still reluctant to relinquish the dependency of their child. The same attitudes present in parents of normal children appear to be exaggerated in parents of handicapped children. In an interview with the foster mother of a mentally retarded child, I asked the woman why she took a handicapped child. Her reply: "Because I was lonely." Because she needs this child, she bucks the system at every turn, thriving on the child's dependence. In this situation the teacher is furnished inaccurate information and insufficient feedback, and the child is truant. While this case is extreme, it is not unusual. The unfortunate aspect is that overprotection devalues the child and denies his educational needs.

Another block to the parent-teacher relationship is the parent who has little interest in his child. Early in my career in special education I had a bitter lesson in this area. As the instigator of a summer recreational program for handicapped children in a good-sized city, I had engaged the cooperation of the entire community. We obtained buildings, materials, volunteer helpers; planned detailed programs; and sent out notices to parents of all the handicapped children on the superintendent's roster. On the opening day, we were ready for seventy-five children. Three came. That night we hastily set up a transportation system, and I determined that in the future this would be the first step. In asking why some parents do not seem to care, through the years several answers have become apparent to me. Some parents may not understand the value of educational programs; others may not agree with the philosophies of a particular program nor feel it is worthwhile (as educators, we find this difficult to accept!). In some cases one has to say, "This is part of the child's problem—his parents *don't* care."

In addition to the overprotective parent and the uncaring parent, there are many parents who want to contribute to their child's education. There are parents who have skills that would be valuable assets to the teachers and to many children. There are parents who could assist professional educators in reaching and teaching less able parents.

There has been a reluctance on the part of schools to admit that they need help. This concept is certainly changing, for with the admission of all children, administrators and other personnel are having to assume tremendous tasks; they are ready to accept any help available. The inflexibility of schedules, personnel, and facilities *must become* a thing of the past. Certainly administrators are becoming more aware of the needs of exceptional children. I was delighted with the attitude of a principal who was approached about admitting a severely handicapped child to his school. His immediate response was "We want to serve all school-age children in the county. Will you help us plan for him?"

A final factor that is detrimental to the parent-teacher relationship is the reluctance on the part of the teacher to accept the abilities of the parents. Since I was a parent before I was a teacher, I readily relate to this idea. There have been so many times I wanted to say:

> I have a son who is retarded.
> I taught him to walk, to use the bathroom,
> to feed himself, to say his first words,
> to interact with the family.
> I know my son; I can help you to know
> him and to teach him.

My suggestions were never welcomed. I was enthusiastically encouraged to help with the field trip to the airport and to make popcorn balls for the Christmas party. And yet, during periodic visits to the classroom, I saw teen-agers wasting valuable time taking naps, obese children constantly snacking, my son learning things he had known five years before. As a parent and as a teacher, I knew these practices were educationally unsound. Perhaps the threat to the teacher is that the lack of good educational programming will be discovered.

In examining the problem and contemplating solutions, there appear to be two factors crucial to parent-professional interaction and effectiveness: communication and respect. While these elements are essential to any good relationship, they seem to be missing in many of our parent-teacher confrontations.

No school program can be maximally effective without carry-over in the home. This requires constant contact and communication between the two settings. Several years ago I was asked to talk with a parent group at a nearby private school for retarded children. My function was to provide a setting for interactiaon between the teachers and the parents. During the ensuing information exchange, one of the teachers described the effectiveness of the toilet-training program. A vocal parent exclaimed that she wished *her* child could be toilet trained. The amazed teacher declared, "But your child *is* toilet trained!" Following the meeting, the teacher and the mother got together and outlined a strategy for continuing the school program in the home. They also planned future conferences to discuss further developments in the child's education.

In an early experience as a special education teacher, I was led to an understanding of the importance of communicating with the child, of including him in discussions about himself. We had assembled a child psychiatrist, the school principal, the mother of the child, and me, to try to resolve Mike's severe emotional problems. The psychiatrist immediately asked why Mike was not present. I was amazed at the suggestion and said so. The doctor replied, "Doesn't he know we're talking about him? If you were in that position, wouldn't you rather be on *this* side of the door?"

Communication which includes the teacher, the parents, and the child is a rewarding experience. The focus of our summer camp program was to help prepare severely handicapped children for school. In assessing the needs of a charming, verbal, severely physically handicapped child, we found him to be overbearing and sometimes abusive in making demands on people. We could see this behavior as his chief handicap in the school setting. The parent conference included him, his teacher, both parents, his brother, and his sister. We related our observations, backed up with a video-tape record of offensive behavior. The parents readily saw the problem, as did the child. As a team, we worked out a strategy to help him improve his own behavior. Such planning avoids confusion and misunderstanding; it establishes good communication.

Communication can be facilitated; respect has to grow. Parents of handicapped children are subjected to constant humiliation; it is incredible that much of it comes from persons engaged in the "helping" professions. One learns to deal with the impudent stares of strangers ("You seem interested in my son; would you like to meet him?"). One expects more understanding from persons claiming to be experts in areas of exceptionality.

My good friend and I attended a conference concerned with educating severely handicapped children. Both of us were there as college professors in special education and as parents of retarded children. As we listened intently to one of the major speakers, we heard him say, "This book would be valuable to parents of retarded children, since it is written on an eighth-grade reading level."

The current concept of *parent training* is extremely insulting. Some of my colleagues told me of an encounter with a young mother and her two boys, aged seven and twelve, both mentally retarded and blind. My associate suggested that parent training was indicated. I wondered at the time who we knew who could tell this mother *anything*. In fact, I immediately wanted to meet and learn from a woman who had raised children with such complicated problems. Since that time I have had the distinct pleasure of working with her and her children. We pooled our resources; we learned from each other. Parent training? This mother and father were good parents long before I came along.

Part of the block to understanding and respecting parents may come from the age-old, hopefully changing idea that the professional person knows everything. We have particularly elevated the physician and the college professor into positions of unerring wisdom.

I returned to college after my children were in school. Although older than my fellow students, I was in awe of my teachers. One morning after I dropped my son, who has Down's syndrome, off at his class and visited with the boys and girls there, I made the trip to the university to attend a class in speech and hearing. The professor, in discussing speech development of the retarded child, made the profound statement: "There are no mongoloid girls."

Somewhat later, in a course related to curriculum for the retarded child, the professor, who had had years of experience teaching retarded youngsters, declared, "Retarded children have no imagination." I returned home that afternoon to find my retarded son riding a "horse" he had constructed from a chair, some blankets, and a rope.

The thought began to develop that I knew more about some things than the professionals did. I began to gain confidence in the knowledge I had gained as a *parent*. Years later, I am still convinced that I have learned more from my own children than from any other resource.

Members of the medical profession seem to be particularly deified. My first disillusion came when we learned what the distinct features of our child implied eighteen months and five physicians after his birth. It is now inconceivable to me that such ignorance (or cowardice) could have prevailed. The sensitivity of the pediatrician who did reveal the facts to us almost obliterated our negative feelings.

Years later, as an educator, I had an experience which further revealed to me the fact that physicians are human and do not, cannot, know everything. I had been asked to evaluate David for probable placement in a special class. He had been having difficulty for the four years that he had been in school. A battery of tests and consultation revealed that his measured intelligence was below normal and that he would probably profit from special education. Convincing his mother was another thing; it was finally accomplished and David was placed in a special class where he began to blossom under individualized instruction. David's mother then took him in for a routine physical examination and, after a ten-minute examination, was informed, "This child is not retarded." David was taken from the special class.

Recently a friend of mine who is a nurse and I took a youngster to a physician for some advice. We asked a particular question, to which the physician replied, "I don't know." The nurse looked at me and whispered, "Didn't that sound beautiful?"

While I have been offended as a parent, I have also been rebuffed as a teacher. I have found that many parents think that no one else knows their problems, no one else has experienced their heartaches, that no one understands. In conferences with the parents of the children I taught, frequently they would say, "But you don't know what we go through." While I could empathize on one level as a parent, I also was angered as a teacher because in many cases the teacher spends more time with the child than the parent does. To say the teacher does not understand is insulting. Sometimes the teacher spends hours outlining remedial or developmental procedures which should be continued at home. In many cases, it is obvious that the procedure has not been followed.

Parents need to demonstrate their respect for the teacher and the school. One teacher asked me, "May I spank your son if I think it's necessary?" I was taken aback for a moment, then quickly thought that if I was leaving my child in this teacher's hands, it had to be completely. I answered yes, and although I don't believe she ever spanked him, she knew that I respected her judgment.

Respect for the child is, of course, the essential bond between the parent and the professional. When I was in graduate school, I happened to be sitting in the coffee shop with a friend when a young woman stopped by our table. A friend of my companion, she had just graduated in special education. When asked what she would be doing in the fall, she replied, "Oh, I'll be teaching a bunch of nuts over at Fifth Avenue School." My son was one of those nuts. It was not a good year for him; his teacher had no respect for him; she expected very little from her students and got exactly that. How could I respect her?

By contrast, my son had one teacher who expected him to learn. She was hard on him; he had homework, he had to learn parts for class plays, he had responsibilities in the classroom. He also had an entry in the community science fair, won a state-wide art contest, and discovered that he could read. This teacher, in one year, accomplished more with my son than the accumulation of the other years produced. She respected him; she valued him as a person who was capable of learning and of accepting responsibility. She valued me as a parent but let me know that she had everything under control in the classroom.

Is there any way to resolve the conflict existing between parents and professionals working with handicapped children? There has to be. Most of the negative incidences I have related occurred through ignorance or thoughtlessness. The parents and the teachers simply do not seem to be aware of the lack of communication and respect that is sometimes felt. Awareness, therefore, seems to be the starting point.

During my first experience of working with severely handicapped children, one incident indicated some potential for creating empathy between parents and teachers. For ten days, teachers and children lived together, ate together, slept together, and learned together. At the end of that time, one young man (a psychologist) said that he had gained tremendous respect for teachers and for parents; living with children with overwhelming problems made him very sympathetic with people who would be dealing with them on a daily basis. He further revealed that he had seen patience and kindness in the teachers that he had not known existed. At the same time, the teachers expressed a tremendous empathy with the parents. As an example, we had observed marks across one child's back on the first day and speculated that he had been whipped. We were aghast, but at the end of the ten days; after discovering how very difficult and obnoxious this child could be, we wondered if we would not also beat him if provoked. Sleeping in the same room with a child who gets up repeatedly or eating with a child who throws his food gives one a very deep sense of compassion for the families who do it every day. Interestingly, when the parents came for conferences, they were delighted with the gains the children had made; plans were made to continue the work at home. Parents, teachers, and children were concerned for each other; they were working together.

There are many programs being instituted for the preschool handicapped child and for the severely handicapped child. These programs rely heavily on parent-professional cooperation. Perhaps this reliance can be generalized to other areas of exceptionality. As we grow in our understanding of the needs of the child, hopefully we will realize that the handicapped child is dependent on the cooperation of his parents and the professional persons who are concerned about him. Awareness of our individual problems, our unique abilities, and our strength as a team will facilitate that cooperation.

References

Cain, L. F. Parent groups: Their role in a better life for the handicapped. *Exceptional Children*, May 1976, 432–437.

Kean, J. Successful integration: The parents' role. *The Exceptional Parent*, 1975, October, 5, 35–40.

Mary S. Akerley

Mary S. Akerley is a former teacher who has been active in local, state, and national affairs of the National Society for Autistic Children, having served as its president and presently serving her seventh year on its board of directors. She is a member of the Maryland Developmental Disabilities Council, and the National Association for Mental Health and Consortium Concerned with the Developmentally Disabled, among other groups. She was also a member of the Maryland Department of Education. She is now Assistant Director for Services, Center for the Handicapped in Silver Spring, Maryland. Her son, Edward Michael, is twelve years old and autistic.

False Gods
and Angry Prophets

It's hot and sunny, a magnificent day. We're on our way south on I-95, heading for the National Society for Autistic Children conference in Orlando. It's a perfect setting for thinking back because if it weren't for Eddie, none of us would be here enjoying this particular drive, in this particular place, on our way to a delightful vacation.

The four kids are, of course, all wearing tee shirts expressing their individual allegiances to some cause, place, or rock group. But so are Mom and Dad, and I think that's significant because I doubt very much that we could have brought ourselves to do something so "undignified" without Eddie's help. John is an engineer, I'm a former English teacher, and Eddie is our youngest child—he has autism. Autism is a very traumatic but effective cure for caring too much about what other people think of you. It is perhaps the ultimate liberator.

My tee shirt has two very nasty-looking vultures on it; one is saying to the other: "Patience My Ass . . . I'm Going to Kill Something!" The shirt was a gift from an NSAC friend, another member of the battered parent club. Most of us, like the hungry vulture, have run out of patience and have struck out for ourselves . . . and for our children.

We don't begin in anger. We start out the way all parents of all children do: with respect, reverence really, for the professional and his skills. The pediatrician, the teacher, the writer of books and articles on child development, they are the sources of wisdom from which we must draw in order to be good parents. We believe, we consult, we do as we are told, and all goes well unless . . . one of our kids has a handicap.

We parents are almost always the first to notice that something is amiss, and one of our early consolations is often our pediatrician's assurance that "it's nothing—he'll outgrow it." That, of course, is exactly what we want to hear because it corresponds perfectly to the dwindling hope in our hearts, so we defer to the expert and our child loses another year. Finally the time does come when not even the most conservative professional can deny the existence of a problem. The difficulty now is to define it and plan accordingly. With luck, our pediatrician refers us to an appropriate specialist and we are (or should be) on our way.

We transfer our trust to the new god and wait expectantly for the oracle to speak. Instead of the strong, authoritative voice of wisdom, we more often hear an evasive stammer: "Can't give you a definite diagnosis . . . uh, mumble, mumble . . . virtually untestable. . . . Let us see him . . . cough, cough . . . again in a year." Ironically, when the oracle *is* loud and clear, it is often wrong: "Seriously emotionally disturbed; it's a severe withdrawal reaction to maternal ambivalence." The parents have just been treated to their first dose of professional puffery, and it is very bitter medicine, all the more so for being almost totally ineffective.

Its one potentially redeeming feature may be realized if the parents react with sufficient anger to take charge, to assert their right to be their child's "case manager." Unfortunately, this is not likely to happen at such an early stage; it takes more than one false god to make us give up religion entirely. And when (or *if*) we do manage to assert ourselves, our behavior is viewed by professionals as the final stage in our own pathology; any of us who may still be practicing religion are immediately excommunicated.

This is not empty theory; we have lived it. When Eddie was still an infant, we suspected all was not right; by the time he was a year old, we were sure. These were not the feelings of our pediatrician, who clearly viewed us as overanxious parents. All he saw was an unusually beautiful child in perfect physical health, who was perhaps "just a little slow." Our difficulties in managing the child were not regarded as significant, even when the setting for a scene was the doctor's office. "I have lots of children in my practice who act like that." Then God help you, doctor, and the children, too!

It took a sit-in on the occasion of Eddie's three-year checkup to convince the man to do something. I had warned the office nurse when I made the appointment that I would not leave the consulting room until I got help, and I held my ground. It was my first act of parental assertion; had it not been successful, my son would probably still be wordless, friendless, essentially lifeless.

We were referred to a pediatric neurologist. Considering what I know now, it was an unusually enlightened choice. For most parents of children like Eddie, the first referral is to a child psychiatrist who considers them, not their child, the primary patients. The neurologist and her colleague, a psychologist, did the best evaluation they could with a subject who was at best uncooperative, at worst totally unresponsive.

The results, however, were singularly unhelpful: "We can't give you a diagnosis; his symptoms don't fit any known syndrome. We've never seen a child like this." John and I didn't know whether to weep or take a bow. I remember trying to pry something more specific from them: "Is he retarded? Autistic? (I had learned the word about two weeks earlier) Disturbed?" All of the above? None of the above seemed more like it; at least none of the familiar labels appeared to hit the mark precisely enough for the pros to be comfortable with it, but in their desire to be precise, they overlooked the need to be supportive. We felt totally abandoned. If they didn't know what was wrong, who would? And if no one knew, then no one would know what to do. Eddie was trapped in his misery, and we were trapped right in there with him.

Perhaps I am being unfair. Autism is a toughie to diagnose; the early signs are subtle, and Eddie had partially lost one of the primary symptoms: inability to relate to people. He had, largely due to my stumbling efforts, become very attached to me—overly so, in fact. Nevertheless, I find it hard to excuse either specialist. Both should have known that autism must be diagnosed retrospectively because most of the children do develop at least a little, and the behaviors Eddie exhibited were not unusual signs of progress in an autistic child. Within a year I learned all that; why hadn't they?

They did recommend we get help from a child therapist and gave us three names. I picked the one most convenient to our home and called her. She was not taking any new patients, but she did encourage me to talk, and something in my tale of woe must have moved her because she took us on. What is more, she helped. Her approach was purely practical: examine a piece of distressing behavior and explore ways of eliminating or changing it. It was a soft form of behavior modification and it worked. On the other hand, she did not shy away from the theoretical; she actually suggested books for me to read and, when pressed, ventured a diagnosis and a rather classy one at that: symbiotic psychosis with autistic defenses. Many years later, when Eddie entered public school and John and I reviewed the mountain of records that followed him there, the only good words about us as parents were hers.

Ironically, it was this genuinely helpful therapist who introduced us to the parent-eating variety. She was a consultant for a special school and managed to get Eddie enrolled there. She continued as his therapist for that school year but with the understanding that we would switch to a staff psychiatrist when the new school year began. In this case "staff psychiatrist" equalled a very green resident, fresh out of Freudian U and, as we later discovered, utterly powerless to deviate from establishment practice even when his or her own common sense suggested it.

So much has been written about the abuse of the parents of autistic children by traditional psychiatrists that even one more word seems superfluous, yet the abuse continues and thus so must the protests. We worked with two doctors at that school (sequentially—we weren't *that* bad!). Neither ever came right out and said, "You caused it," but everything they did say was based on that premise. Our involvement with a parent organization was viewed as a way of avoiding our emotional duty to our child; never mind that he was improving dramatically, in no small part because of what we had learned through that involvement. Our failure to need their kind of help was "blocking"; our by-now angry fighting back, "resistance." The real mind-blower for Doctor Number One was my refusal to admit I hated and resented Eddie because I had had to turn down a graduate fellowship when full-time study would have kept me away from him too much. Doctor Number Two picked up the theme and kept "working with me" ("*on* me" is more like it) to admit my anger. Finally I blew: "You bet I'm angry, Dr. B., and I know what I'm angry at—you!"

Again, perhaps I'm being too harsh. Both of these doctors had had many years of school; neither had ever had a child. Obviously they still had a great deal to learn about the priorities of love. Yet, even now, I cannot write these words without feeling a rage that makes my pen tremble. I am still angry.

The worst professional damage—not to us, but to Eddie—occurred during this time. We took him back to the neurologist for a reevaluation. She had suggested we do so as soon as we felt he could endure all the testing involved. When we advised Doctor Number One of our plans, she came close to losing her professional cool: "You didn't ask my permission! You're going to put him through all that for nothing; you're clutching at straws just to prove it's not your fault! If you go through with this, he can't stay here."

Her diatribe produced a fury in me that was quelled only by her last sentence. Fear took over. There is not exactly a wealth of choices when it comes to schools for autistic children, and this one was doing a good job. We didn't want Eddie to lose this help he needed so badly, but we didn't want him deprived of any medical intervention that could help either. It was a cruel choice, especially since it was so unnecessary and artificial. Thank God we again had the guts to take over and be proper parents. Eddie and I moved into Children's Hospital for three days for the most complete neurological evaluation possible. We had, in effect, called the school's bluff. They didn't want to give up what they had termed, *in our presence*, "an interesting case" (who, us or Eddie?), especially one which looked more and more like a success story. Doctor Number One even visited Eddie in the hospital.

It *was* an ordeal for him, as it would be for any five year old, but hardly the trauma our expert had predicted. And it was well worth the effort. The testing revealed that Eddie was what is now called a purine autistic; that is, his uric acid level was significantly high—two to three times the normal level for a child his age.

There was even an experimental treatment regime similar to that used for gout patients. Naturally, we were eager to begin it; just as naturally, the school was not. They reintroduced the "heads we win, tails you lose" decision-making process by again threatening to expel Eddie if we insisted on allowing the neurologist to treat him. There was no way to circumvent the situation: the neurologist refused to jeopardize a successful school placement for an unproven medical methodology; moreover, the dietary restrictions alone made secrecy impossible. Another factor made cooperation essential: school personnel, psychiatric and educational, were to serve as evaluators of behavioral change.

Our discouragement was relieved slightly by the news that Doctor Number One was leaving and, come fall, we would have a new therapist. The neurologist suggested we wait and hope for a more cooperative, open doctor. As soon as Doctor Number Two arrived, she contacted him to discuss her proposed neurological management. Immediately afterwards, she called us, elated.

"Good news, Mrs. Akerley. It looks as though you got a winner this time. I've just talked to Dr. B., and he's very interested and willing to cooperate."

For some as yet unexplained reason, Dr. B. was too busy to begin seeing us until school had been in session for six weeks. Perhaps it took that long for the school's supervising psychiatrist to indoctrinate him into the proper ways of treating autistic children and their parents, for when we encountered one another at last, there was no support for any neurological intervention—only the hostility we had come to know so well. I wondered then how many times human hope can be crushed before it refuses to rise again. Fortunately, I have yet to find out.

By then I had lost all vestiges of "cooperative patient" and of "tactful human being" as well. The one benefit I had derived from years of enforced therapy was a mouth unrestrained by the graceful social manners my poor mother had worked so hard to instill. Besides, therapy was *my* hour, not his, so I delivered my reaction to his rejection in "plainspeak":

"I don't believe what I'm hearing. You told our neurologist that you were very interested in her work and very willing to participate in her treatment plan for Eddie. She couldn't believe we had finally gotten a cooperative shrink. Now you're giving us an unqualified, unexplained no. I don't believe it's your decision. You're still in training, and you're just doing what you've been told, following the institution line. Is this the way you're going to handle treatment all year? Will you have to get permission for everything you want to do? When do they let you make up your own mind? When do we get to work with a fully qualified therapist? I'm tired of being someone's lab assignment!"

Needless to say, he defended the decision as his own; in fact, he brought it up frequently in the months that followed, but I never bought it. Nor was he too professional for a counterthrust: he quite justifiably pointed out that the only reason we were eager to resume therapy that fall was to get started on the new neurological treatment. I never tried to deny it. John and I had long since given up any hope of real help from therapy and had come to regard our fifty-minute hour as an unavoidable part of the school's tuition. We had found other, more valid sources of help for ourselves, and we had found them all on our own. No professional had ever suggested we join a parent's organization; in fact, they all appeared threatened by such groups and by the growing competence and self-assurance we derived from our participation.

Eddie's therapy (two thirty-minute sessions per week) was a different matter. While he was now speaking, it was typical autistic speech, not useful enough for talk therapy, so he played with toys from the doctor's collection (carefully selected for psychoanalytic potential), and the therapist interpreted his play. Anyone familiar

with the "play" of an autistic child might be tempted to feel considerable sympathy for the psychiatrist and hope his or her boredom threshold was very high. Let me remind any such readers that autistic play
is replete with opportunities for the properly trained observer to see
fixation, withdrawal, hostility, sexual repression, and a host of other
Freudian goodies. And see them they do.

John and I, in our hour, heard some of these interpretations; two
come to mind as excellent examples. Eddie was fascinated by telephone poles; ergo, he had phallic anxieties. The second, I thought,
was considerably more imaginative. One of Eddie's favorite play-
things was a set of wooden dowels that were part of a construction-
type toy. His way of enjoying them was to stand them on end, lie
down, and move his head back and forth behind them. (He played
similar eye games in front of store windows in which basically vertical
items were displayed, not atypical for an autistic child.) I chose to see
his little game (after trying it myself) as his independent discovery of
the theory of relativity; not so the learned doctor, who patiently explained to me that I had clearly kept Eddie in his crib and playpen too
much because he was now reliving the behind-bars trauma! My response was really more innocent than sarcastic, although it was not
perceived that way: "If it was so awful, why is he reliving it with such
obvious pleasure?" No answer came.

If all this psychoanalytic nonsense had been shared only with us,
I probably would have been more amused than frightened. But, because I had seen this type of therapy when visiting other, similar programs, I had every reason to believe that Eddie's behavior was interpreted to *him* as well. For example: "Oh, I see you've dropped the
mother doll. I guess you would like to reject your mommy the way
she has rejected you." I knew his receptive language was up to following this kind of talk, and the possibility of his ever hearing it
frightened me.

If those child therapists really wanted to help Eddie, I believe
they should have tried to make themselves psychologically invisible.
They should have done all in their power to enhance the normal relationships in his life. Instead, motivated by Technicolor rescue fantasies, they charged between a child and the people who loved him
most in an egocentric effort to make themselves paramount.

I remember when Eddie learned to kiss. We had taught him the
mechanics and had been getting back a lifeless touching of his lips to
our cheeks. Then one night at bedtime it happened—a real kiss. I
could hardly wait to report this exciting mark of progress to Doctor
Number Two. At our regular session a few days later, he preempted me
(he had seen Eddie the day before).

"Eddie kissed me," he announced smugly with the most self-satisfied look I have ever seen on a human face.

"Me, too" was all I could say.

"When?" There was actually fear in his voice, and when he heard the answer, he was visibly upset. "That means he kissed you before he kissed me!"

Right, doctor, and that is as it should be.

The entire situation had taken on a terrible irony. Eddie was being denied a treatment which was based on objective, scientific evidence while being forced to undergo a therapy based on subjective, introspective fantasy. Fortunately, thanks to several gifted teachers and a truly creative speech therapist, he had progressed to the point where a change of schools seemed called for. This gave us the courage to contact the neurologist and suggest that treatment begin. Meanwhile, we began looking into possible schools.

Sound medical practice is basically conservative, so the doctor first tried to bring Eddie's uric acid level down by diet alone: no meat, no fish, no nuts, no whole grains, no chocolate, no cola—most of his favorite foods (and a lot of things he refused to eat!) were eliminated. I gave him a simple but honest explanation of why he could no longer have them, which he seemed to understand and accept. (Eventually he got to be better than I at watching his diet.) I sent him off to school with jelly or ketchup sandwiches made with margarine, fruit, plain cookies, and skim milk; I even included food for snack time. I felt excited, hopeful, and, with the expulsion threat defused, invulnerable. I had underestimated Doctor Number Two's resourcefulness. Unable to wait for my next scheduled appointment, he called me at home with a brand-new threat: the diet was going to give Eddie an oral fixation! My response was not printable and, since I did not believe in superstitions, Eddie stayed on the diet and I retained my lovely feeling of freedom. Our child was ours again, and we would make the decisions that we would have to live with.

The diet by itself was not effective, so allopurinol, a drug which inhibits the body's production of uric acid, was introduced. Within a week we had a different child. He began to play with toys in normal creative ways, his language skills took a quantum leap forward, and his behavior calmed down. His teachers (who did not know about the medication) could not believe the difference. We could, because we had always believed that within Eddie lay a great deal of potential that the right treatment would bring out.

That was all a long time ago; the worst, thank God, is behind us. Eddie's new school was a replay of the first but with a more normal academic program, from which he benefitted enormously. And we did not suffer this time because, all our reverence for false gods gone, we no longer doubted our own competence. One day I kept Eddie out for an appointment with the neurologist; the next day I caught hell because I had not asked permission. Would they have felt the same way if it had been a dental appointment? Oh, yes, indeed. Perhaps then it was time to get something straight; did they, by chance, consider themselves the primary case managers? Of course. Well, we did not: that responsibility was ours alone. They were providing a service which we had determined we wished to purchase for our child; we were the customers, we would call the shots. I did not ask permission from my other children's schools to make professional appointments; I had no intention of mothering Eddie any differently.

So our poor therapist would not feel entirely useless, we made up interesting problems for him to work on. We specialized in religious crises, taking our cue from an early session (the second one, if I remember correctly) which he filled with the telling of his own life story. He was an ex-priest married to an ex-nun, and they had not waited for Rome to dispense them from their vows before beginning their life together. I'm still not sure of the reason for this astonishing confession—perhaps to set us at ease, perhaps to challenge us to play "Can You Top This?" We tried. And, since we were not allowed to talk about Eddie, we spent a lot of time on the therapist's children, two boys aged three and five, whom their daddy seemed to have a great deal of difficulty managing.

One day he advised us that the entire staff had observed that we acted like strangers in the waiting room before our appointment (it was 8:00 A.M., for God's sake!), whereupon we graciously offered to make love the very next week if the school would provide a comfortable couch. They didn't, but we were finally excused from therapy with the inspiring words, "Well, you've won! You don't have to come in any more!" Cured, were we? Not really, just vocal. I had been on a fairly well-publicized TV talk show the week before (I was then president of the state chapter of NSAC) and had used the opportunity to blast the inflated costs of private special schools, citing enforced, useless psychotherapy as a prime factor.

Eddie is now in our public school's SLD (specific learning disabilities) program. To be sure, he is still very much on the periphery of life, and that is hard for all of us . . . so near and yet so far. But it is more progress than any of the many people who have worked with him over the years ever dared hope for. We are elated and grateful but I, at least, have not—cannot—forgive those who, instead of helping, added to our pain. I believe there can be no greater sin.

True, we survived, and are stronger, richer people for the experience. But we, and all the contributors to this book, are exceptions. The average parent does not get a chance to speak out in books or on television; he has to sit still and take it. We cannot even always find him to offer help; the chances are 60–40 that he's already gone under.

The people whose words you read here have survived in spite of the professionals, not because of them. There are many lessons for would-be helpers to learn from their stories: respect for parental competence, humility in the face of one's own ignorance, acceptance of the contributions of other professional disciplines; but they all stem from the eloquently simple tenet of the physician's code: Do no harm.

Elizabeth M. Boggs

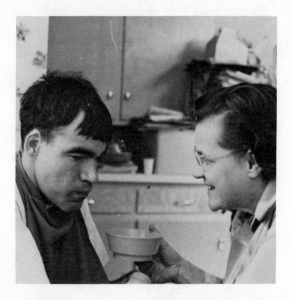

Elizabeth Boggs, a volunteer advocate for the cause of the mentally retarded since 1950, chose full-time involvement in issues of legislation and public policy in preference to a career in applied mathematics. She was one of the founders of the National Association for Retarded Children in 1950, and in 1958 became its first woman president; she served as chairperson or member of its Governmental Affairs Committee from 1965–71. She also served as a member of President Kennedy's Panel on Mental Retardation in 1961–62 and the National Institute of Health National Advisory Council on Child Health and Human Development from 1961–71. She completed terms as chairperson of the National Advisory Council on Services and Facilities for the Developmentally Disabled and as a member of the President's Commission on Mental Retardation. She is currently a member of the Technical Consultant Panel on a Minimum Long-Term Care Data Set for the National Center on Health Statistics, and also chairs the Task Group on Implementation of Rights of the International League of Societies for the Mentally Handicapped.

Her son, David, is profoundly retarded and multiply handicapped, and is a resident at the Hunterdon State School, about five miles from her home near Clinton, New Jersey. His father, Fitzhugh W. Boggs, died in 1971.

Who Is Putting Whose Head
In the Sand
Or in the Clouds
As the Case May Be?

As this tale unfolds it will be increasingly clear that my son is not only handicapped but disabled by anyone's criteria, including those of the Social Security Administration. Thus, my qualifications as a parent are unimpeachable. My qualifications as a professional in the field of mental retardation, however, are a matter of courtesy. Unlike Phil Roos, I was not a professional in the human services field before I was a parent; unlike Elsie Helsel, I did not go after another degree in special education; unlike Rud Turnbull, I did not have a profession I could turn directly toward the field to which my parenthood called attention. Only indirectly did my training in the discipline of science (my doctorate was in mathematical chemistry) help me in the early days to understand the limitations and constraints on the methods of the biological sciences and hence to serve for a while as an interpreter between those scientists and the parents who were eager for miracles from the laboratory.

In these days when certificates, diplomas, and guild membership cards are so often required as passports to participation in decision making, I am heartened to be able to report that I have only rarely been put down or excluded from human policy deliberations in which I judged myself competent. Moreover, I have been permitted to sit and learn in many situations where I would not presume to speak, except to ask questions. To the ever-increasing body of professionals, especially those in universities and in government, who have permitted me to be productive in roles for which my credentials were distinctly unconventional, I owe, and warmly tender, sincere thanks. This is one respect in which my relationships with the professional community over the past quarter century have been exceptionally gratifying.

I am also fortunate in being old enough to have escaped the overbearing coercion of modern feminism which tends to judge productivity by the standards of the marketplace. I am proud to be the only person who has been continuously active in some volunteer capacity within the National Association for Retarded Citizens since I participated in its founding in 1950. I believe that NARC has a unique role to play, and that the existence of a strong collective lay advocacy group which continues to recognize and respond to the great diversity of need among persons called retarded is the single most essential element in securing their future. I have jealously guarded my amateur status within the association even when positions as a consultant and lecture fees have come my way on the outside. In the early days I carried out many unbudgeted assignments which are now executed by paid staff. In recent years I have been able to accentuate multiple linkages with other agencies and movements which no one with ties to a paid position could have made. The "cause" has taken me to forty-four states, plus Puerto Rico and ten foreign countries. It is hard to put a job title on the role I've played. One could say that I've been a social synergist with a predisposition toward communication and collaboration rather than confrontation.

That's the public or "professional" side. What of the private, the personal, the parental side? As we are all fond of telling each other, each person, each parent, each family experience is unique; yet there are common themes. How many of us, like Phil and Susan Roos, were told that we were overanxious, that our child's tardiness in meeting milestones was within normal limits? How many of us who founded local associations and organized the classes and recruited the executive directors now feel with Janet Bennett that local ARCs are no longer places where parents feel useful? How many of us like Tot Avis have seen the doctrines swing and now speculate about the potential orthodoxy of the eighties? Is still another perspective of any value? In an effort to give some integrity to this essay, I've selected some personal vignettes which I relate to three themes of concern to me: first, the discrepancy between the intents of public policy and the actualities of life for retarded individuals and their families; second, the mismatch between research findings and both public policy and private practice (these themes are related, as it happens, to the work of the two NARC committees on which I have had the most extended service); third, the recurrent professional and societal denial of the differentness of the most disabled, and their resultant need for their own ergonomic (Note I) environments.

This derogation of deviance may have as a secondary effect an unnecessary and inappropriate isolation of those people who, in fact, come face to face with this deviance as immediate care givers. It's not for nothing that a new magazine of growing circulation is called *The Exceptional Parent* or that George Tarjan (director of the Neuropsychiatric Institute, U.C.L.A.) considered it a major victory when the attendants at Pacific State Hospital were no longer reluctant to reveal where they worked.

Out of my personal experience, I've picked four vignettes to illustrate these themes. They deal with the *crisis, daily living, the right to education*, and the *institutionalization of deinstitutionalization*. I still live with the last theme as a current issue; my personal experience with the other three goes back a quarter of a century, but something tells me things haven't changed all that much.

The Crisis

Jonathan David Boggs was born on August 25, 1945. The date is significant for two reasons. It was the second Saturday after V-J Day and, as such, was the first Saturday on which my husband Fitzhugh Boggs had not put in a full day (eight to five) at the laboratory. Therefore, when I began having early labor pains about six o'clock on the morning of the twenty-fifth, it was not necessary for us to grapple with the decision as to whether or not he would go to work.

Some eight weeks before, I had resigned my own research job at the Explosives Research Laboratory at Bruceton, Pennsylvania. That was after V-E Day and after our group at the laboratory had completed its technical contributions to the design of the implosion device being put together at Los Alamos. At the Westinghouse Research Laboratories in East Pittsburgh, Fitzhugh had researched some of the radar jamming technology which had helped the Britons to win the Battle of Britain. At the time, neither of us knew what the other had contributed to the war effort.

We congratulated ourselves on our timing. It may have been more critical than we realized. With the end of the war, penicillin, which had previously been limited to use in military hospitals, was released for civilian use. When David was ten days old, he became very ill. He had a high fever and a nervous twitching referred to as tetany. Several possible hypotheses were advanced as to the cause of the illness. Our pediatrician later told us that in all his considerable experience he had seen only one similar case. That child had died. An autopsy had shown an infection entering by way of the umbilical cord. David was treated with penicillin and survived. Many years later I was to address the Ways and Means Committee of the U.S. House of Representatives in support of extended authority for the Maternal and Child Health Program. My theme was "Survival Is Not Enough." Since then, a collaborative perinatal study supported by the National Institute of Health has yielded a technique for examining the discarded cord in the delivery room to detect such infections.

It was a harrowing three weeks. Dr. Gerald Caplan (1960) at Harvard has studied family crises of which ours was undoubtedly a classic example. As a crisis it was, I believe, well handled by the professionals. We were permitted to express our worries. No one denied the gravity of the situation. The physicians gave us their full attention and took care to explain the reasons for their several tentative diagnoses. They described the treatments, including a period of continuous lavage. A cousin of mine who is a registered nurse saw us through the transition from hospital to home which otherwise would have been still more frightening to me. David began to regain weight, and the doctors foretold no after effects.

But that was not the real crisis. The real crisis unfolded over the next twenty months. David first approached and then gradually—almost imperceptibly at first—fell behind the normal developmental timetable. When he was eight months old, our pediatrician asked us, apparently casually, whether we thought he could hear. We said we did not know. In fact, we were not sure until he was more than two years old when he responded to the sound of running bath water.

In the spring of 1946, David spent a month in the care of an aunt while Fitzhugh and I vacationed in Cuba where my parents were living at the time. Fitzhugh was between jobs, and it was the only opportunity we ever had for four consecutive weeks of vacation. If I had known then what I know now about critical periods of separation for infants, I would have arranged things differently. However, while we were away, David learned to roll over.

During the next ten months we were nomads. This was the immediate post-war era, and housing was at a premium. We had purchased a house in Upper Montclair, New Jersey, but were unable to evict the tenants (our legal effort to do so was put off by a technicality). As a result, David and I saw a succession of pediatricians. Each of them responded reassuringly to my description of his slow progress. When he was a little over a year and barely standing, the pediatrician with whom I had hoped to settle down answered my query with "Well, he's prehensile, isn't he?"

In the face of being told repeatedly that David's progress was satisfactory, I did not share my own misgivings with Fitzhugh. As it turned out, he had his own. I seldom dream, or, to be more accurate, I do not recollect the dreams I have. Fitzhugh, by contrast, used to have consistent recurring dreams whenver he was confronted with a continuing problem. As he told me afterward, he had been having such dreams, always about David. They stopped immediately when we found a pediatrician who, without prompting from us, indicated that we had a problem.

It was only a partial resolution, however. Having delivered himself of the judgment that David might be self-supporting in a lowly occupation, he was not willing to assist us to obtain further medical consultation. I suppose he saw us as "shopping" parents. If so, it was a misjudgment on his part because we, in fact, were very grateful to him for admitting to the reality which we ourselves observed; namely, David was not developing at a normal rate. However, he resisted our request for a psychological evaluation and for further consultation on the medical side. Because of our appreciation, we felt considerable loyalty to him, and it was hard for us to break away. But eventually we did so, in order to obtain a comprehensive evaluation at Babies Hospital, the pediatric hospital associated with the College of Physicians and Surgeons in New York City. The doctors recommended institutionalization. By this time David was nearly three.

Following the findings of Dr. Caplan's (1960) studies of families in crisis, I see that this crisis, from our leading questions through an adequate analysis and reasonable exhaustion of remedies, was not well handled by the professionals involved. One would like to think that times have changed since then. Unfortunately, the word still has not gotten around. A young attorney friend of mine, well-acquainted with the field of mental retardation professionally, gave birth recently to a baby in a major Washington hospital. Tentative suspicion of Down's Syndrome on the basis of inspection was conveyed to her and her husband, but she had to fight to get a confirming cytogenetic study carried out. We also still hear reports of routine advice for instant institutionalization at birth.

Daily Living

We accepted the findings of the physicians' and surgeons' group as to the severity of David's impairment, along with its nonspecificity. We also accepted the notion that the underlying organic cause was not directly subject to remediation. (While putting himself through college, Fitzhugh had worked as a lab technician in a research department of neurology, and he had a rather vivid firsthand understanding of the effect of lesions in the central nervous system.) We did not, however, accept the group's advice to proceed with institutionalization. We were reinforced in this decision by David himself who gave us his response to the three or four days of hospitalization. As we got into the car, preparatory to leaving the hospital, he stood between us on the front seat and speechless as he was and is, gave us in body language the unmistakable message "Let's get the hell out of here!"

He lived with us until he was nearly seven. They were trying years in which we were largely on our own. Nevertheless, our efforts toward toilet training and self-feeding were to a considerable extent rewarded. But they were also years in which we could find no means to convey instructions or guidance to him about behavior which was either dangerous to him or productive of chaos in the household. His destructiveness did not convey a sense of rebellion or anger, but rather a total lack of comprehension that it was unacceptable to us. One had to be present physically to deter him from running into the street, destroying the neighbors' flowers, tearing up the magazines in the living room, removing the contents of the refrigerator, and getting up at night and pounding on the window just to hear the noise. Unfortunately, the neighbors also heard the noise and complained to the police.

I do not want to convey by this recitation that his motor development was normal. Indeed, by the time he was four, it was apparent that he had a mild cerebral palsy. Since then, this disability has become more apparent, and his contractions are now so severe that he walks a hundred feet with considerable difficulty.

The problem at that time, however, was one of accommodating extraordinary stress in the family's daily activities. Up until that time I had been a fairly meticulous housekeeper. However, the work of tidying and cleaning could be undone in thirty seconds by David's activities. In addition to caring for David, cleaning up after him would have been a full-time job, had I elected to do it. However, I saw the necessity for maintaining some time for my own intellectual pursuits as well as some outside activities, and we began to tolerate a high degree of disorder in the house. We removed most of the bric-a-brac and became resigned to the scarring of our furniture.

I had, by this time, postponed more or less indefinitely the notion of going back to professional work. I joined the League of Women Voters, a step that turned out to have been particularly useful since it taught me some important things about the operation of state government in New Jersey. I also began taking occasional courses at what was then the Newark State Teachers College, now Kean College of New Jersey. The clinical psychologist who gave the course "Introduction to Tests and Measurements" told me about a clinic being organized by the brand-new Essex County Unit of the New Jersey Parents' Group for Retarded Children. This was truly a self-help group, and its dynamics were very different in those days than they are now that the professionals have largely taken over. But that is another story which I shall not tell here.

Rather, I wish to make some restrospective observations about this period from the point of view of support to parents and the prevention of parental burnout. Michael Bayley (1973), in reporting some sensitive British studies, documents the effects of the daily grind on families who retain a retarded member at home for many years. These deleterious effects can, in part, be mitigated. Christine Maslach (1976) has recently reported studies on burnout among various types of professional personnel who give direct care or service. These include social workers, child-care workers, attorneys, and others who constantly confront the insoluable problems of other people. Generally speaking, the confrontations of the professionals are limited to working hours. Even so, Maslach's research indicated that uninterrupted hours of direct contact, along with isolation from peers having similar duties, were factors in the vulnerability to such stress. She points out that when the stress becomes intolerable, the professional is likely to respond in one of two ways. He or she either cops out or begins to depersonalize the clients or patients and to blame them for their own misfortunes. Cop-out is possible, for example, when the social worker goes back to graduate school and takes a degree in administration. Both copping-out and depersonalization by staff work to reduce professional productivity are detrimental to those being served. Maslach's findings suggest that limiting the duration of periods of exposure through planned direct contact and opportunities for peer group interactions can help to reduce burnout and thus enhance humanization for both care giver and care receiver. Although these studies did not include parents as subjects, it is fairly clear that there is a parallelism and hence a lesson to be learned and applied.

In retrospect, I can see that we in our situation had managed to apply some of these principles. We had what we referred to as a built-in baby-sitter. Having bought an old house with a third floor, we took advantage of a temporary post-war lifting of one-family zoning restrictions to create a small apartment there for a service man and his family. The apartment was rent-free to them as long as they were available on an intermittent and irregular but mutually agreeable schedule to look after David in our absence. This permitted us not only to go out for an evening (which included participating in parent group meetings) but also to intersperse daytime routines with brief intermittent absences.

This model of respite care is, I believe, closer to the mark for both mother and child than is the all-day day-care center or the occasional fortnight of residential care which is more likely to be offered today. Quite frankly, I believe that we have not yet come to grips with reconciling what we know about the need of a child for a continuing and uniquely identified parent figure on the one hand, and the need to prevent burnout and to foster personhood in parents, especially mothers. I am speaking particularly of the first three or four years of the child's life. The National Collaborative Infant Project developed by the United Cerebral Palsy Association, with the cooperation of NARC and others, has demonstrated a model of early intervention which could displace group day-care for most very young handicapped children (Haynes, 1977). Quite aside from the services to the child, it combines assistance to mothers to enable them to be more effective parents, with brief spells of relief from the extraordinary demands of parenting a handicapped child. Both natural parents and foster parents need these supports. The significance of the high turnover already being noted among house parents in group homes should be studied against this hypothesis.

The Right to Education

The charter members of the Essex unit were a remarkably foresighted lot. By the time Fitzhugh and I came on board with them late in 1949, they had organized an interdisciplinary diagnostic clinic, to which a hardy band of professionals were contributing their time. The initial applicants were accepted by age groups so that the needs of a group could be identified for service planning. Soon there were enough six to nine year olds identified as trainable to justify organizing some classes. This was my first volunteer organizational task. Two classes were opened in October 1950, one in a Sunday school room, the other in a neighborhood house.

These children had been denied admission to local schools. However, we had a social mission in mind, so we, too, had some eligibility criteria. The children had to be toilet-trained and able to understand simple commands. Our mission was to persuade the county superintendent of schools, and through him the local superintendents, that such children could respond to skillful teaching in a classroom setting in a manner that invited accommodation in the public schools.

We were, in fact, going backward to the practices of the period from 1911 to 1930 when "imbecile" children had been accepted and provided with an approved curriculum in the larger communities in New Jersey. A state department of education publication of 1918 prescribes sense training, speech training, manual training, and "exercises of practical life." It then goes on to note "while results with this group are crude, the improvement in children is marked" (Anderson, 1918). It is hard to re-create now what these classes developed by the Essex unit meant to parents as well as children.

In connection with my duties, I enjoyed my first experiences of "professional" acceptance. I was permitted to sit in on the clinic team conferences at which recommendations were made relative to those children to be referred to me for class placement. I learned a lot from this, particularly as I was able to review the individual reports and watch the children they described over a period of time. It did not take me long to conclude that David would not be eligible for these classes.

About this time the neighboring local unit (Bergen-Passic) organized a summer day camp. Its admission standards were not as demanding as our classes. They claimed they could handle "anyone." The director urged me to send David, implying that my reluctance was an expression of overprotection. We agreed to give it a try, but some weeks later when I visited, I found David off in an enclave by himself, doing the same things as he did in the play yard at home.

But meanwhile I was also caught up in the group strategy to obtain legislation which would admit the children in our classes to public school, with a program suited to their needs. I became chairperson of the State ARC Education Committee. We studied the state constitution [" . . . a thorough and efficient system of public schools for the instruction of all the children in the state between the ages of 5 and eighteen years . . . "] (Art. VIII, Sec. IV, Par. 1) and the law [" . . . courses of study suited to the age and attainments of all pupils . . . "] (N.J.R.S. 18:11). Exclusions were permitted for contagious disease or behavior dangerous to others, but there was nothing about excluding pupils based on their IQ. Here again was that invisibility—that denial of the existence of exceptions. Suffice it to say that our strategy worked. In 1954 the governor signed a mandatory special education law (N. J. R. S. 18:46), replacing the one enacted in 1911 (the first in the nation), which had been rendered inoperative in effect by the school administrators. They had done so by labelling children with IQs below fifty as ineducable. Our use of the word "trainable" enabled us to accentuate the positive without getting into a confrontation on the issue of the three Rs. Our efforts were paralleled in other states.

A national movement was under way. By 1952 I was chairperson of the NARC Education Committee. In 1954 NARC published a policy statement recommended by the committee, which I quote in full below:

AN EDUCATIONAL BILL OF RIGHTS FOR THE RETARDED CHILD

Every child, including every retarded child, is important and has the right to
1. Opportunities for the fullest realization of his potentialities, however limited, for physical, mental, emotional, and spiritual growth;
2. Affection and understanding from those responsible for his care and guidance during his years of dependence;
3. A program of education and training suited to his particular needs and carried forward in the environment most favorable for him, whether in the public schools, a residential center, or his own home;
4. Help, stimulation and guidance from skilled teachers, provided by his community and state as part of a broadly conceived program of free public education.

And his parents have the right to determine for themselves, on the basis of competent advice, the course of care, training, and treatment, among those open to them, which they believe best for their family; and to have their decisions respected by others. (NARC, 1954)

When I was president of NARC (1958–60) and Gunnar Dybwad was executive, I suggested that we republish the preceding statement and give it a bit more play. When this did not happen, and I asked why, I was shown a letter from the current chairman of the Education Committee, who stated the opinion that the statement was unrealistic, that the schools would not accept the most severely and profoundly retarded, and that we were jeopardizing our chances for the trainable by making such sweeping demands. Perhaps she was right; despite the burgeoning literature about schooling for the profoundly retarded and zero reject, I still perceive some invisible children. In fact, when the director of a recent federally funded project asked for nominations of innovative programs for the very severely and profoundly retarded, he had to reject about half of them as not dealing with what the project had in mind. Even NARC once sponsored a film in which a typical child with Down's Syndrome was described as profoundly retarded. Anyway, Dr. Dybwad felt constrained to refrain from reissuing the 1954 policy.

The Institutionalization of Deinstitutionalization

Let me now skip, chronologically, to the present day. David is now thirty-two. He does not understand instructions, let alone any conversation which might enable him to anticipate what is going to happen. He has learned, however, to recognize a variety of situational clues. For example, certain observable activities precede mealtimes. The regularity of routine in daily living is therefore of considerably more significance to him than it would be were he able to receive oral or written alerts anticipating changes in that routine. He cooperates in the activities of daily living in which he is not entirely self-sufficient. It is thus important for him to be assisted by people who are well acquainted with his capabilities and his signals since he cannot tell them how to help him. Consistency by care givers and continuity of staffing are especially important for people whose disability includes the absence of communication skills. This is the best protection against "learned helplessness" (DeVellis, 1977).

David likes to eat, rock in a rocking chair, swing in a playground swing, ride in an automobile, and get into water, whether it be a shower or a swimming pool. There is a limit to the amount of time he or anyone else can spend in these activities, and, therefore, I must assume that he is bored or tuned out a good deal of the time, especially in the winter.

At the 1977 American Association on Mental Deficiency convention Dr. Burton Blatt gave an exquisite illustrated talk on the current documentation he and two colleagues have done on the state of affairs in institutions as contrasted with the state of affairs ten years ago (Blatt, 1977). There has been considerable progress, but his final message was that the people in institutions are lonely. One got the impression that loneliness is a function of the institution and that people in the community are not lonely. Subsequently, I made some observations in the hotel lobby. I was looking for a seat, and all the seats were occupied. With one or two exceptions, no one was talking to anyone else, and all of the people looked as solemn and as lonely as those in Dr. Blatt's film. There are a great many lonely people out in the community, and many of them are in foster care, group homes, boarding homes, nursing homes, and even in families. I would be lonely myself if I did not have the motivation, skill, energy, and independence to seek out contact and communication with other human beings. I think I would be particularly lonely if I were assigned to live with a small group of people not of my own choosing.

David's group is not small, however. Most of the members of the group of men with whom he lives are more capable in one or another respect than he. However, neither they nor he fit the nursing care model (those who need constant care from semi-skilled staff). Some can talk a little; others can take advantage of the craft instruction which is offered. David does not participate, not only because he does not have the manual dexterity but because conceptually the product does not have meaning; and the process is not pleasing. The more capable men may leave the cottage alone and move about the grounds of the institution on their own recognizance; David must be escorted. On his own he would soon be on the highway or in the woods. One of the more capable men has selected David for paternalistic attention. Charlie sees to it that David gets his own chair back when it has been usurped by another. Charlie's advocacy is both expressive and instrumental. David benefits, but he does not really reciprocate. Indeed, there are very few people for whom David reserves his own enigmatic but gleeful smile. One of these is a young woman who was working as a cottage training technician while putting herself through college. It is a mark of the improvement of the way our institutions are run that she was permitted to express a little favoritism towards him.

She is now raising her own son. Recently she visited David while he was in the local hospital following some surgery. As the two of us watched him together, she mused, "I often wonder what he is thinking about, how the world looks to him." That thought is too infrequently pondered. If he were his own architect, how would David design his environment?

There are some parents who like the idea of normalization (Wolfensberger, 1972) because it is useful in glossing over the realities of difference. I sometimes think there are professionals who like it for the same reason. Rather than trying to create a "normal" environment for my son, I try to think of how the world must look from his point of view, and what kind of an environment would not only minimize his boredom and loneliness but enhance his sense of dominance. When I try to put myself in his skin, I realize that he, like me, has an immediate environment, a home; that is, the place where he sleeps, eats, and spends his leisure time with certain associates, and an immediate external environment which is called the community. His home environment could be improved from his point of view by reducing the noise level created by a really extraordinary architectural anomaly, reducing the size of and the number of people occupying the same daytime living space at the same time (i.e., subdividing the space appropriately), and reducing the total number of staff and residents with whom David has some interaction, provided this could be done in such a way as to retain in his "family" those people he would most like to have with him, while at the same time increasing autonomy and reducing the risk of burnout for the caregivers. (The particular residential facility in which he now resides still maintains an overly hierarchical as distinct from a colleague pattern of organization of the direct care staff.) All this could be done equally well in any residential unit whether on campus or in the community.

But what of the community environment? The "community" surrounding David's "home" is the campus of the state school. It is an ergonomic community; that is, one which has been planned to suit the inhabitants. Its swimming pool is designed so that any one can stand up in any part of it. There is a twenty-mile hour speed limit on all its roads. Its doctors make house calls. Its respite care arrangements are always available, that is, when the parent surrogate has an emergency, another one is available. There is a restaurant where no one stares at the sloppy eaters. Nobody there thinks that it is inappropriate for a thirty-two-year-old man to use a swing on the playground by choice; it is not considered dehumanizing to let a man act like a child if he wants to. David is not restricted by any such environmental taboos.

From his point of view this community is more facilitative and more enhancing than the town half a mile down the road. There were times in the past when I deliberately escorted David into my community. Because he does not like to be in the water where he cannot put his foot firmly on the bottom of the pool, the area of the community swimming pool actually available to him was very small. On the public beach he would trample the neighboring family's picnic because he wanted their banana. The nurses in the general hospital put him into an enclosed crib (normal for children) which was too short for him. Being integrated into the community means nothing to him. Perhaps we should consider ways of making the community more aware that people with his extreme problems exist and need special care and attention. But first, I think we have to persuade the armchair policy-making professionals of their very existence.

How can we describe their extraordinary need for an adaptive environment structured to their requirements rather than ours? We need some new terminology, it seems. In a recent large meeting a well-known superintendent, who runs a facility in which there are residents like David, remarked that they had recently placed a number of profoundly retarded adults in the community, and that when these "profoundly" retarded adults were asked whether they would like to return to the institution, they all said, "No." I am sure that the adults to whom he referred were successfully placed, and I do not doubt their capacity and the voluntariness and lack of coercion in their expression of preference. If people who could make such a conceptual choice, who could understand the question, and express an answer are called profoundly retarded, then we need some new term for those who cannot do any of these things.

Richard Willis (1973) did a time sample study in the late sixties of the interactions of the men residing in a residence hall for the severely and profoundly retarded. These men were able to move about; a large number of behaviors were coded. Unexpectedly, Willis observed that the men seemed to fall into two groups: those who exhibited a variety of behaviors scattered over all segments of the range; and those who failed to exhibit a large but discrete cluster of behaviors, many of which hinged around the area of communication. Willis observed that the absent behaviors appeared to be those which psychologists generally ascribe to homo sapiens but not to other primates. He called this group of residents noncultural. For this honest observation he received at least one derogatory review.

In discussing normalization, Wolfensberger (1972) has emphasized that many norms are culturally determined. Normal behaviors and normal settings are therefore not absolutely meritorious. Even the rhythms of life may vary from one society to another. Since cultures are created by and for the convenience and comfort of the members of a particular society, it would appear that subcultures are not only permissible but, for some purposes at least, ought to be encouraged. Successful societies are students of ergonomy; they fit the habitat to the inhabitants. If the inhabitants differ from one another, then so should the habitats and even the subcultures, ethnic or otherwise. In an era of divergent life styles, it seems particularly ironic that we place such stress on normalization for the retarded. Somehow the gap between public policy and private preferences seems great at times. Social reforms based on theoretical constructs are still pursued with the same missionary zeal as was the eugenics movement in times past.

I spend a great deal of time in Washington pondering the language of legislation and the rubrics of regulations. Most of the time I am working for the disabled, the retarded, the majority, but sometimes I try to relate what goes on there during the week with what I see when I bring David home on the weekend. Of all the things I have done to influence federal programs in the last twenty-two years, there are very few to whose impact I can trace any improvement in my son's well-being, although there have been improvements. There is one exception. In 1969 I helped to initiate the sequence of activities which led to the Intermediate Care Facilities/Mental Retardation (ICF/MR) legislation in 1971, and thus eventually to the controversial ICF/MR regulations of 1977 (Note 2). It seems likely that within the next two or three years the facility where my son resides may become an ICF/MR.

Ironically enough, I do not anticipate that this will bring about the improvements which I believe would be most conductive to significant recent research findings by a number of investigators working in various settings, on aspects of organizational structure and staff-resident interactions. (See, for example, Zigler and Balla, 1977; Raynes, 1977; Pratt et al., 1977; Moore et al., 1976; Wheeler, 1977.) The ICF/MR federal regulations deal with ratios of beds to rooms and staff to residents; although they may increase the direct care staff by a few additional positions, they will not change the way in which the staffing is organized or supervised. If the number of beds in David's bedroom is reduced from six to four, it will not make any difference to him. It will not change the layout of the day room or improve its acoustics (Gentry & Zimring, 1977). He will acquire an individual written habilitation plan. His case will be reviewed on paper somewhat more frequently, and this will raise the per capita cost, but little will change back at the cottage. Charlie will probably be classified as eligible for community placement in a group home, and he will leave. He will not have David to be concerned about. David will miss his defense against the more bossy residents, who will remain because their behavior will not be found acceptable in the group home.

Recently I was invited to give a talk at the NARC convention. I aired some of my concerns as a parent of a multiply handicapped, profoundly retarded adult son (Boggs, 1976). Nothing I have said or written in the past thirty years has occasioned such an outpouring of letters and comments by other parents. Some have adult children at home; others are parents of retarded persons who reside elsewhere. Several of these parents pointed out that they had spent many hours during the last ten or twenty years serving on local or state ARC boards, working for community services for children younger than their own, or working for legislation to aid the more numerous more able retarded, while the different needs of their own profoundly handicapped sons or daughters received less insightful study and attention. As Tot Avis has pointed out, it is difficult for parents who have accommodated themselves (perhaps reluctantly) to one professional doctrine to reverse directions when an apparently new doctrine supercedes. The parents who wrote to me, however, are not defenders of the status quo, nor are they sheep. Emotionally, they would like to see the son or daughter they know so well miraculously exhibit the capacity to move like his or her siblings into a life of "freedom and participation," to quote Burt Blatt (1977).

But what is "freedom"? What is "participation"? Is it freedom to be placed in a group home? Is it freedom to be allowed to make by default a vital decision that has consequences foreseeable by others but not by the maker? Is it participation to work for a wage you do not earn on a job where your fellow workers are politely tolerant but quickly exhaust any commonalities of interest in conversation? Is it freedom to be forced to have and follow an individual habilitation plan?

These are questions to be addressed honestly by self-styled advocates for the retarded. But there is also the question of freedom and participation for their families. What parents are saying is "We are being ostracized, segregated, put down, for thinking unorthodox thoughts, for expressing the idea that an environment designed for normal people may not be the optimum for everyone."

In the early fifties, when NARC was very young, it still took courage for a parent to admit to having a retarded child, so great was the stigma. Although some professionals knew better, the public still thought that the child reflected some bar sinister on the family escutcheon, a streak of degeneracy (Note 3). One of the great contributions made by Pearl Buck and Dale Evans Rogers, each of whom wrote books about their experiences as mothers of retarded children, was to enhance the self-image of parents; if these celebrities admitted without shame to having retarded children, then so could lesser folk. Although not in that league, my husband and I both recognized in the mid-fifties that we could fend off the blows fatal to other more vulnerable parents by using those Ph.D. degrees as shield and buckler. But it required some stamina, even so, to uphold a minority position to affirm that retarded children can be helped. Twenty-five years later it still does, even though the majority view we challenge may be different. Now the shield and buckler is not a rather irrelevant doctorate, but a personal examination of the right of one individual to be different, and of one parent to differ—and to be heard.

References

Anderson, M.L. Curriculum for classes for defectives. In State of New Jersey. Department of Public Instruction, *The teaching of children three years or more below the normal*. Trenton: State Gazette Publishing Co., 1918.

Bayley, M. *Mental handicap and community care—A study of mentally handicapped people in Sheffield*. London: Routledge & Kegan Paul, 1973.

Blatt, B. The family album. *Mental Retardation*, 1977, *15*, 3–4.

Boggs, E.M. A volunteer's story. *Mental Retardation News*, 1976, *25*(10), 4–5.

Caplan, G. Patterns of parental response to the crisis of premature birth: A preliminary approach to modifying the mental-health outcome. *Psychiatry*, 1960, *23*, 365–374.

DeVellis, R.F. Learned helplessness in institutions. *Mental Retardation*, 1977, *15*, 10–13.

Gentry, D., & Zimring, C.M. Acoustics and noise affect speech discrimination. R.C. Knight, C.M. Zimring, W.H. Weitzer, & H.C. Wheeler (Eds.), in *Social development and normalised institutional settings — A research report*. Amherst, Mass.: University of Massachusetts, Institute for Man and Environment, 1977.

Haynes, U. *Review of the collaborative project — Monograph #6*. New York: United Cerebral Palsy Associations, 1977.

Maslach, C. Burned-out. *Human Behavior*, 1976, *5*, 16–22.

Moore, H., Butler, E.W., & Bjaanes, A. *Careprovider characteristics and utilization of community opportunities for mentally retarded clients*. Riverside, Calif.: Center for the Study of Community Perspectives, 1976.

National Association for Retarded Children. *The educator's viewpoint*. New York: NARC, 1954.

New Jersey. Constitution of the State of New Jersey, 1949, Article VIII, Section IV, Paragraph I.

New Jersey Revised Statutes, 1952. Title 18, Chapter 11 (now Chapter 33).

New Jersey Revised Statutes, 1955. Title 18, Chapter 46.

Pratt, M.W., Raynes, N.V., & Roses, S. Organizational characteristics and their relationship to the quality of care. In P. Mittler (Ed.), *Research to practice in mental retardation — Care and intervention* (Vol I). Baltimore: University Park Press, 1977.

Raynes, N.V. How big is good? The case for cross-cutting ties. *Mental Retardation*, 1977, *15*, 53–54.

Wheeler, H.C. The direct care staff. In R.C. Knight, C.M. Zimring, W.H. Weitzer, & H.C. Wheeler (Eds.), *Social development and normalised institutional settings — A research report*. Amherst, Mass.: University of Massachusetts, Institute for Man and Environment, 1977.

Willis, R.H. *The institutionalized severely retarded*. Springfield, Ill.; Charles C. Thomas, 1973.

Wolfensberger, W. *The principle of normalization in human services*. Toronto: National Institute on Mental Retardation, 1972.

Zigler. E., & Balla, D. The social policy implications of a research program on the effects of institutionalization on retarded persons. In P. Mittler (Ed.), *Research to practice in mental retardation — Care and intervention* (Vol 1). Baltimore: University Park Press, 1977.

Notes

1. According to the International Ergonomics Association, *ergonomics* is a word coined in 1950 from two Greek words, meaning the "natural laws of work." It is an interdisciplinary science dealing with the basic and applied aspects of human factors in work, machine control, and equipment design.

2. The term *intermediate care facility* was introduced in 1967 when Congress sought to define a level of institutional care less than skilled nursing care but more than room and board. In 1971, Congress permitted public institutions for the retarded meeting certain specific standards to be eligible for medicaid reimbursement under this rubric.

3. In the early part of the century, the great leaders in the field of mental retardation—Fernald, Tredgold, Goddard—perceived feeblemindedness as a discrete entity, but they also observed a more than chance coincidence in the same families with drunkenness and promiscuity. In the early fifties, it was customary to write off their observations as "methodologically unsound." In the past five years we have discovered that there is indeed a fetal alcohol syndrome; some obervers are also concerned that an increase in unmonitored teen-age pregnancies may once again make congenital syphilis a significant cause of mental retardation.

Leah Z. Ziskin

As a public health physician, Leah Ziskin is the director of Parental and Child Health Services in the New Jersey State Department of Health. She is in charge of planning and organizing programs whose goal is to prevent mentally and physically handicapping conditions and to serve handicapped children. She is a fellow of the American Academy of Preventive Medicine and has published in the maternal and child health fields. Leah's nine-year-old daughter, Jennie, is severely mentally retarded, ambulatory, and nonverbal.

The Story of Jennie

Jennie is our third child. She was planned and very much wanted. I had taken care to practice personal preventive medicine before my husband and I decided to have Jennie. I was thirty years old, visited an obstetrician, and was told that I was in good physical condition to have a baby. My concern was prompted because my husband and I had known ABO incompatibility, and we were also Rh incompatible, I being Rh negative. Our first son did not have any problems; however, our second son had jaundice related to our ABO incompatibility. I also checked with a pediatrician at the hospital where I would deliver and he assured me that the hospital was equipped to handle a hematological problem which any infant of ours was likely to have. Having checked out my health and being assured that potential known problems of our infant could be handled, we very happily proceeded to have our third child.

My husband, a physician with a master's degree in biomedical engineering, was working on an Air Force Base in a research capacity in audiologic research. I was a physician working in the occupational health division of the base. My duties included examining airmen

coming back to work following sick leave, handling on-the-job emergencies, and doing examinations on dependents who were staying on
the base. I was also becoming involved in true occupational health
problems related to workers on the base. I worked from 8:00 A.M. till
noon, at which time I went home and cared for my two sons who were
three and one and a half years of age. I was involved with the neighborhood where we lived, because we were away from our family, and
so I felt more like the "normal mother and homemaker" than a professional woman than I have at any other period in my life.

I remember being acutely aware when I knew that I was pregnant
that much of a homemaker's exposure to infectious disease comes
through her children. She is directly and intimately exposed to her own
children and to other children coming to her home who may have
infectious diseases. She may be caught in the secondary spread of
diseases which her children pick up in nursery schools or day-care
centers. She is directly exposed to infectious disease in supermarkets,
on public transportation, in department stores, and in theaters. My
own anecdotal balance of the situation was that a homemaker who is
probably thought not to be at much risk compared to those in oc-
cupations such as nurses and teachers, from an infectious disease
standpoint, had every reason to be concerned; and the medical profession had every reason to be concerned about the homemaker.

Nevertheless, my pregnancy would be considered uneventful; I
felt very well, and I remember thinking that this baby must be all right
because I did feel so well. My life was not overly stressful because of
my limited professional hours and my complete enjoyment or satisfaction of being with my two children without being pulled from them
by professional responsibilities. I therefore looked forward very much
to the birth of our third child.

The baby was delivered without difficulty. I was awake, and the
obstetrician told me that although the baby was small, she looked
healthy. The pediatrician would watch her very closely, but the
medical staff were not overly concerned. Her weight was five pounds
eight ounces, a pound smaller than my two previous children. The one
very disconcerting fact the obstetrician told me, without alarm, was
that the placenta was small. He did not elaborate on any details of the
placenta. Jennie was small but appeared normal to my professional
and maternal eyes.

Within a few weeks after Jennie was born, we were scheduled to
leave Ohio and the Air Force behind us, and return to our home and
families in New Jersey. Jennie had a stormy course those first few
weeks of her life. She had severe respiratory track infections, to the
degree that early one morning I insisted that my husband drive us to

the base hospital because I was afraid Jennie might need a tracheotomy in order to breathe. In retropsect, a great deal of her problem may have been due to small air passageways. But at that time we did not suspect, and the physicians were not cognizant of any unusual congenital difficulties. She recovered without the need of a tracheotomy, and we were able to move the family back to what we considered our permanent civilian home.

Once we were settled and unpacked, I began to be increasingly concerned with my new infant. She just wasn't as active as my previous two children. She was not smiling as early as I would have liked. She just "wasn't right." I measured her and was concerned at her head size. I took out my textbooks and studied tables of growth and development. When it became obvious that Jennie's head size was below or less than that expected for a baby of her chronologic age, I tried to console myself that it was because her birth weight was low. I started making my own ratios of head size to birth weight and head size to length, which were statistics I could not find in any pediatric growth and development tables. I also excused her slower rate of development on the slow recovery from the respiratory syndromes which she had had.

I took Jennie to a pediatrician when she was eight weeks of age. He was a friend of mine, and I distinctly remember saying that I was greatly concerned and worried that Jennie was microcephalic. The pediatrician examined Jennie in a routine fashion—including measurement of her head, measurement of her chest, her length, etc.—looked up at me, and said, "Gee, Leah, you really don't have anything to worry about." This somewhat offhanded reassurance made me feel better for two or three days after which time all my own inner doubts and fears returned.

Every day I looked for Jennie to smile a little, to perhaps start turning, to squirm more in her crib. She was fussy, she was colicky, she had trouble moving her bowels, but all these things I could overlook. I was deeply distressed because what I was expecting to see as developmental landmarks were not appearing.

At this time, I was also job hunting. I finally decided that I would work in the city of Camden in public health clinics. At these clinics I worked examining children, giving immunizations, giving advice and recommendations to mothers of preschool children. Every time I went to a clinic, I looked at these poor, mostly healthy babies and other preschool children, and I would compare them to my newborn daughter. I would pick up a bouncing baby two to three months of age and was so acutely aware of the deficiencies of my daughter's development that it was hard not to think of my deep feelings of personal concern for my own infant. I kept thinking that at home I had a baby who would be offered nutritious foods, who would be adequately clothed, who would have a room and crib of her own, who would have prompt medical attention when she needed it. Here I was looking at babies whose mothers had love for their infants, but who had to struggle to provide clean baby shirts, formulas, cereal, and solid foods. I would rush home from clinic sessions and examine Jennie and again look for signs of development which would somehow assure me that Jennie was as healthy as the lovely babies I had just examined. I was always disappointed. I finally called another pediatrician with whom my husband and I had gone to medical school, and after I described my fears, I ended with, "What should I do?"

This friend recommended that I take Jennie to the pediatric neurologist at one of the children's hospitals in Philadelphia. I knew this neurologist and saw him shortly thereafter. He examined Jennie very thoroughly, and when he finished the exam, he looked at me and said, "We may have a problem." At that point, all my hidden fears of the past few months were realized. Even though he had put it in the realm of probability, to me he certified or validated all the nightmares and the fears I had tried in vain to believe were imaginary. It was the start of the year and a half of what I refer to as my grief period.

The laboratory tests which the neurologist ordered were not extensive. Taking Jennie for the tests, however, I viewed for one of the first times since her birth other abnormal children in a group, and I kept thinking, "Jennie is not like them. Jennie does not belong here." But I knew or sensed that Jennie was like them and that she did belong there. The tests and the neurologist's diagnosis were that Jennie was microcephalic. The tests, however, did not delineate any etiology.

It was a difficult period of time now to tell the family and friends that our lovely baby daughter was not normal and could never be expected to be normal. What was extremely difficult was explaining that we did not know the extent of the abnormality and that even the specialists to whom we took Jennie would not predict the extent of her abnormality or what deficiencies we could expect. I, therefore, taught myself to expect the worse. I imagined that she might live in a crib, that she might be completely dependent. I thought back to severely retarded and abnormal children I had taken care of during my internship and at other times I had worked in hospitals, and I had nightmares of what my child would be.

The worst statement or the statement that evoked the worst emotional response in me was "Don't worry, dear, everything's going to be fine." It took every ounce of will power and every lesson in tact and diplomacy that I had ever learned to contain myself and not shout back at anyone who said this, that I had reason to worry and that things were not going to be fine.

During this period, I mentally went back over my pregnancy. I mentally reviewed what I did, persons I was in contact with, what types of exposures I possibly had to things that could not be tested for. I tried to calculate how much radiation I might have been exposed to. We had bought a large order of meat from a supermarket, and I theorized that the meat might have had preservatives which might have affected my child. I had used cyclamates which had not been removed from markets at that time, and I thought this might be the cause of my child's abnormality. None of my theories could be proven, and I was enough of a scientist to know that I was just torturing myself.

I reminded myself that I had taken great care in being prepared for this child, and I, therefore, tried to blame my husband in some way. My husband let me do this for a very limited period and then smartly reminded me that we were in this together and that it was no more his fault than it was mine and that he was not going to carry the blame or the guilt any more than I should.

In an attempt to try to get me away from my problem, my husband took me on a convention trip with him to Toronto. I remember on that long drive through the mountains of New York State and Canada, feeling that I had become a completely different person. I felt my ego had been wiped out. My superego with all its guilts had become the most prominent part of my personality and I had completely lost my self-esteem. I felt I was nobody. Any credits of self-worth that I could give myself from any of my personal endeavors meant nothing. Graduating from college and a first-rate medical school, surviving an internship, practicing medicine and having two beautiful sons and a good marriage counted for nil. All I knew at this point was that I was the mother of an abnormal and most likely retarded child.

It took about a year until I came home from working in a clinic and said to my husband, "Today I had a problem that was greater than Jennie." My very wise husband said, "That must mean you're getting better." It did mean that I was getting better, but it took a few more very painful months, and easily another two years, until I believed again that I was more than the mother of a retarded child. I decided that I did not want the major distinction of my life to be that I was the mother of a retarded child. I finally was able to pick up the pieces of my life and proceed.

Once I knew Jennie was retarded, I actually resisted going to organizations or other people for help. I don't know why I felt this way. I did think that they might not understand my particular situation or I would not feel comfortable in a group. Perhaps some of these feelings were because I was accustomed to giving advice in a professional capacity and much less accustomed to receiving counseling. Thus, although I knew organizations existed, I refrained from joining them.

When Jennie was about fourteen months old, I attended a pediatric seminar at a local hospital. On the program was an internist who described a school for trainable retarded children. He came to this pediatric meeting not only to make physicians in the locale aware of this resource but also to look for physician volunteers to participate in a school health program. I took this opportunity to introduce myself to the speaker and volunteered to participate in the school health program. I then ventured that I had a child who had a problem and asked for more information about the preschool program he had briefly described. The doctor was perceptive and proceeded to tell me that he was involved because he and his wife also had a retarded child. The school helped both Jennie and me greatly. The school had one of the few infant stimulation programs in our area, and it was held on Saturday mornings, which made it possible for Jennie and me to attend. While volunteers from local high schools, colleges, and other interested persons worked with the children, the parents met separately. We heard lectures on various topics related to retarded children. Some of the topics concerned genetics, feeding practices, and delayed growth and development. Some of the parents had special concerns or looked into the latest medical literature. One of the theories of the time was that high doses of vitamin B_6, pyrodoxine, were very beneficial to children with Down's syndrome.

The school was run by an extremely dynamic priest and a core of brothers, all from Ireland. Their brogue was delightful and their spirit comforting. We all hoped our children would learn to speak with Irish accents.

The group attending the school was largely Catholic; however, there was no attempt to limit any of the activities of the school in any way to one religious sect. However, the general philosophy of this school was Catholic. I learned that our children were "special," that God granted special strength and had special concern for these children and their families. I thought this was a beautiful philosophy which was comforting to many people, although I did not feel I should be chosen for any special strength. I looked for similar philosophies in other religions, but did not find it as a clearly defined philosophy.

About this time, I recalled that Pearl Buck had had a retarded child and that she had written a book about her own experiences. I found her book, *The Child Who Never Grew*, and read it. What impressed me was that it took her so long to accept the fact that her child was retarded and that she consulted physicians throughout the world in an attempt to find a diagnosis that she could accept. I had to compare my own experiences with Pearl Buck's because many members of our family and many friends had questioned my husband and me about why we hadn't sought many more medical opinions. Why hadn't we gone to New York, Boston, Texas, California, or the Mayo Clinic in an attempt to seek a more favorable prognosis for our child or to seek the best possible care or treatment to improve what she might be? The only way that I can explain why we did not seek multiple consultations regarding Jennie's diagnosis was that we actually perceived something was wrong with our child. We then sought a reputable medical facility and reputable physicians highly qualified or specialized in this field. We tried very hard to listen to what they said and to understand what they told us. I truly believe that the physician we did consult could not tell us exactly what was in store for us or how Jennie's life was going to be. He could not do this because he did not know. I can understand how professionals do not know and how very often parents think that professionals are probably trying to hide things from them or don't want to tell them facts, but in all honesty, even the most highly knowledgeable professionals cannot give clear-cut, well-defined answers. I personally feel now, although I did not at the time, that the parents will have to see their own child evolve to appreciate his own unique growth and development.

There are many schools of thought concerning intensive therapies, many of which are done in the home. Our philosophy was that we wanted our home to remain a home. We had two other normal children to consider, and these children did not deserve to have their home and their world revolving around another child who was different. We thus consciously elected that nothing special or that no elaborate therapies be done in our home. We also consciously elected to put the needs of our two normal children first. We felt that their potential in life warranted and justified more of our time and more of our effort. I realize that all families with retarded children or children with special problems cannot make this decision as easily as we could or as consciously as we did. We were aided in making this decision because we were told by highly qualified specialized professionals that if we provided a stimulating environment for Jennie and if we gave her love, care, and consideration, she would grow and develop at her pace and reach her potential. Therefore, our conscious decision was perhaps easier. We wanted to believe what the professionals told us.

There was a time when I was haunted by the thought that if Jennie were to be dependent all her life and eventually might have to be put into an institution, why was I waiting for this time? Why was I allowing myself to grow to love her, to care for her? Why shouldn't I give her up now before these ties of love developed? A very dear psychologist who tested Jennie finally helped me resolve these questions. She explained to me that she thought our home environment gave Jennie a sense of well-being. She could also learn social skills and how to get along with people, which would serve her well throughout her life whether she remained with us or whether she eventually had to be cared for outside our home. This psychologist explained to me that children who were ambulatory, who could eat by themselves, who were toilet trained, or who could dress themselves probably received better care and more attention than children who could not do these things if they ever had to be cared for in an institution. The fact that Jennie knew how to smile, knew how to love other people would serve her very well in any situation if we personally could no longer care for her. This way of thinking about what we were doing for Jennie and how we were helping her at home would thus be very valuable preparation for her graduation from home. It gave me a better outlook and made me think that her staying at home was meaningful to her total development.

Jennie has learned to walk. She started walking when she was four years of age, and it was more than just her own accomplishment. The school helped, her brothers helped, our housekeepers helped. Jennie climbs stairs, eats with silverware, sits at the table with us, and drinks by herself. Jennie is now nine, and we hope her next major achievement will be that she gets toilet trained. In return for our efforts, Jennie gives us love and a sense of patience. She makes us see that all people do not learn or progress at the same rapid rate. She makes us appreciate the gift of speech, the gift of communication. She makes us marvel that she communicates with us in her own way. She communicates by going to where things are, by going to the drawer where the cookies are, by going to the refrigerator when she wants a drink, by perking up when she sees her coat.

Our life style is different because of Jennie. I felt that I had a problem that I accepted to the degree that I was not paralyzed or impeded by it. The days of getting up in the morning and wishing that she were not there were gone. I had in my medical training collected data and in my practice was aware of cases of sudden infant death syndrome. In this syndrome, infants with no prior illness are found dead in their cribs. Autopsies reveal no definitive cause of death. I almost wanted or wished to experience sudden infant death syndrome as a mother. I wished it would happen to my child. After I realized that it was not going to happen, that every morning I woke and went into Jennie's bedroom she was going to be there alive, I realized that the family and I would have to compensate and compromise and that we would have to live with Jennie. It didn't turn out as badly as I thought it would in those early days. We were able to have outside help because both my husband and I worked. The outside help proved to be beneficial because I could return to practicing my profession without worrying about my normal sons and my abnormal daughter during the day.

I think that Jennie influenced my decision to go back to school and specialize in public health because I was more aware that people with special problems needed support from government-sponsored programs. The problem need not be just that of a retarded child. The problem of poverty, lack of accessible health care, and inadequate housing were problems that I felt I wanted to work to help alleviate. Public programs certainly benefit Jennie. Jennie now attends a state-sponsored day training center. She is picked up about nine in the morning and delivered home about four in the afternoon in a mini-bus. At her school, she is taught social skills that we help her carry through at home. She is taught to improve her walking and table manners; she is also being toilet trained. She is taught sit-ups, tumbling, and exercises. It is a great thrill to me that when she is absent for a period of several weeks because of an especially resistant cold, I get a note that Jennie is missed at school. She gets report cards which are funny because they so often mirror her behavior at home.

We have had to make adaptations in our lives because of Jennie. We have rationalized that these adaptations are good for the family and that we are happy with them, and we don't even think we have made them because of Jennie. One example that comes to mind is our acquisition of a cabin or summer house as we call it. Our favorite vacations used to be finding a cabin in a wooded area away from civilization. It was always difficult to take Jennie because we had to cart cribs and other paraphernalia not knowing what we would find or where we would settle ourselves. We therefore decided that it would be so much easier for us if we had our own cabin already stocked with the equipment we all wanted. After diligent searching, we found a cabin in woods an hour from our home. It is now one of the main forces that keeps us a united family and is a great source of inspiration and a joy to all of us. In a sense, we have to thank Jennie for making it more difficult to travel and for prompting us to find our own cabin.

Jennie's brothers requested that I include these thoughts:

My name is Daniel. I'm twelve years old, and we live in a nice neighborhood in a fairly large house. I think Jennie knows our house and recognizes things in it. She has a great capacity for associating things with activities. For instance, if she sees somebody get a coat from a closet, she will know that they are leaving the house. If she sees me, she starts giggling because she knows that I like to tickle her and play with her. If she sees different bottles, she'll reach for one beside the other even if I switch the bottles around. I think Jennie is very cheerful most of the time, except at night she is sometimes cranky.

My name is Alan. I am ten years old. I am very impressed and proud of my sister's accomplishments in walking, going up and down the stairs, eating at the table with the rest of the family, and especially understanding simple commands. You can also tell her feelings by her expressions. For instance, if someone puts his coat on to go outside and leaves without taking her, she gets very upset. Also, you can tell if she likes some foods or if she doesn't like them by her expressions—if she spits it out, you know she doesn't like it!

Judy Burke

Judy Burke has a master's degree in early childhood special education and is currently employed as coordinator of the Infant Treatment Group at the Division for Disorders in Development and Learning at the University of North Carolina at Chapel Hill.

Her daughter, Becky, is now in the second grade at Frank Porter Graham Elementary School in Chapel Hill, North Carolina. She has cerebral palsy and is beginning to walk.

Face to Face in Times of Crisis and Over the Long Haul

As the Indian drums throbbed in the night air, something was happening in my body at the same time. When the drums reached their crescendo, I noticed that a pain was shooting through me. I was almost seven months pregnant, and my husband and I and our two adopted Indian children were visiting our Crow Indian friends at their encampment during the annual summer powwow. I realized that something wasn't right about those throbbing pains. Although our friends pressed us to stay the night with them because they did not want me to make the fifty-mile trip in my condition, I felt that I must get home. I didn't tell anyone why I wanted to get home because I was afraid that if I verbalized my feeling that something was wrong, it would be true. I hoped that if I got home and slept, I would feel better in the morning.

After we got home I slept a little but the pains became more convincing. By 8:00 A.M. they were quite definite and by 9:00 I knew it was time to call my obstetrician. I spoke with the nurse and described my pains; she said that I should come in and be checked because I had had a miscarriage the year before. She said that it was probably

83

just contractions and gave me an appointment for that afternoon. Suspecting that I would be away from home for some time, I cleaned the house and arranged with my neighbor to care for my two boys (ages four and eight).

As she sat drinking coffee with me, my neighbor watched my face anxiously for signs of the pains. She tried to explain what real labor pains are like, so we could figure out if this was false labor. We laughed at ourselves for sitting calmly drinking coffee with a crisis under way.

My husband nervously hurried around trying to help me and to understand the situation. He took me to the clinic when it was time for my appointment. Meanwhile, the pains had continued to come every five minutes for several hours. When I saw the doctor he said, "What seems to be the trouble?" I answered that I hoped he could tell me since I had no experience at having a baby. He snapped angrily that he couldn't tell me anything until I told him what was the matter. After I explained about the pains, he examined me and then rushed to the phone with his rubber gloves still on his hands. He called the hospital across the street and told them I was coming in about to deliver prematurely. I heard him mumbling into the phone as I struggled to get my slightly bulky body out of the uncomfortable position it had been in while he was examining me. I heard him say, "Eight centimeters." Not knowing what this meant I could tell from his voice that it was bad. He turned from the phone and said that I must go across the street to the hospital immediately. He asked how he could reach my husband, and I replied that he was in the waiting room. He called Bill in and told him that I was about to deliver the baby and to get me right over to the hospital.

We arrived at the hospital about 2:00 P.M. and within a few minutes the hospital personnel had bustled and flapped me into a bed in the labor room, where I was left alone to lie and think for a couple of hours. I was calmly terrified, but after quietly lying for a short time, the pains began to subside and diminished in intensity. At 5:00 P.M. the doctor came in and stood at the foot of my bed discussing current events from the news with my husband while I lay there feeling like a nuisance and an incompetent baby-maker. Finally the doctor said he was going to break the water and get things moving. I wondered why we were trying to get things moving when it seemed to me that they would do better not to move for another couple of months, but I didn't say anything. I had to trust him.

Becky was born at 6:41 P.M., and the nurse and the doctor told me that she was a girl and seemed pretty strong. After a few procedures they took me to my room. On the way we stopped by the nursery, so I could look at her. She was in an isolette which was to be her home for the next two months, and she looked wonderful to me.

The days and weeks that followed were filled with confusion and fear. The pediatrician who cared for Becky was very cautious and pessimistic when I asked questions about her prognosis. He told me that she had some problems with her heart and respiration.

She weighed two pounds thirteen ounces at birth and she lost weight down to two pounds seven ounces. As the weeks progressed, we visited her each day at the hospital and looked at her through the window of the nursery. The nurses would push the isolette into a position that allowed us to see her. They would come out into the hall and talk to us about how she was doing.

During this time she had many crises, and the doctor had explored several possible reasons for her difficulties. He was hampered by a lack of facilities and personnel. At that particular time in Billings, Montana, there was no equipment and no specialist who could diagnose or treat an infant with acute cardiac or respiratory problems. Since Becky was so tiny and was having so much difficulty, the doctors didn't feel that she could be taken to Seattle, Salt Lake City, or Denver where such facilities and specialists were available. Therefore, they just kept trying to figure out what could be causing her to breathe so irregularly and to stop breathing occasionally (almost every day).

Sometimes when I made my daily phone call to the doctor, he would tell me that he didn't think Becky was going to live through the day. The first time this happened I called Bill at work and asked him to come home and take me to the hospital to see her. When we arrived at the hospital, I asked him to please go first and see if she was dead. He came back looking puzzled and said that he saw her lying in her isolette as usual and no one else around in that section of the nursery. We went back together and there she was looking pink and beautiful as usual (naturally, I always thought she was beautiful even though she was extremely thin at first). Finally one of the nurses came out and saw us looking in the window. She came out and told us that Becky had had a very bad spell that morning and they had had a very difficult time reviving her but now she was breathing all right.

The nurses who cared for Becky during her seventy-five days in the hospital were a major source of support and strength to me. One, whose last name was also Burke, told me that she thought Becky was stronger than the doctors thought and that all they could do was support her until she grew strong enough to survive on her own. The encouragement and hope these nurses gave me enabled me to remain convinced that Becky would make it. They told me about her accomplishments as well as her spells. They were always excited to report her weight gains. This seemed very important to me. They were so obviously interested in Becky and me. I couldn't thank them enough for the care they gave her. Sometimes I baked brownies or something and took them up to the nurses' lounge, and in other ways I tried to show consideration and appreciation for the important things they did for us. I feel that in a relationship between parents of handicapped children and the professionals who help them, mutual respect and supportiveness are important. I want them to be good to me, so I try to be good to them.

When Becky was about two months old, the doctor began to be more encouraged and told me I could come to the hospital and feed her. She weighed over four pounds by that time, and he said she could go home when she weighed five pounds. The nurses were so kind and friendly to me that I felt quite comfortable with them and with my tiny, pink daughter when they placed her in my arms.

I had never had a baby before, so Becky's small size didn't seem abnormal to me. When we took her home, she weighed five pounds one ounce and was two and a half months old. Another piece of good fortune helped keep me relaxed about Becky. Although she had had many crises, I had never been present when they happened. This made them seem unreal to me; consequently, I wasn't afraid to take her home and treat her as normally as possible.

When Becky was one year old, we moved to Gainesville, Florida. Our pediatrician in Billings had sent a letter of referral to Shands Hospital at the University of Florida. Our first visit to this large teaching hospital for Becky to be examined by the pediatric cardiologist and another, later visit to the same place for an examination by the pediatric neurologist are among my worst memories.

We arrived at the hospital at 8:00 A.M. and spent the whole day there. I filled out pages and pages of forms and questionnaires as I juggled my wiggly daughter. We were sent from this lab to that with instructions to "go to the third floor, turn left at the desk, go down three doors, turn right, and hand these cards and this form to the girl at the desk there," etc.

About 10:30 A.M. we were finished with all the lab tests and were told to return to the pediatric cardiology clinic. There we were placed in a small examining room and I was told to undress Becky again and wait for the doctor. At 12:30 I went out to the desk and asked the nurse if we could go and get some lunch. They assured me that the doctor would come soon. A little later after Becky had drunk several bottles of water (I had brought only one bottle of juice for her) and wet all the diapers I had brought for her, I asked the nurse to hold Becky for me for a minute. I couldn't lay her on the table or the chair because she'd fall and the floor was too cold to put her there. The problem was that I had to go to the bathroom and I didn't think I could manage it with Becky in my arms. The nurse grudgingly agreed but insisted I must be back in one minute. This episode increased my already rising feelings of anxiety and helplessness in this cold, impersonal place.

About 1:30 the resident physician came in and listened to Becky's chest and asked me some questions. He mentioned that she had a heart murmur. My fear and nervousness increased. At 3:00 the cardiologist came in and examined my sleeping daughter. She called the resident in and asked him to listen to Becky's heart again and said "Where's your murmur now?" I hoped she was the one who was right.

After the cardiologist finished examining Becky, she told me that she had a normal EKG and her heart was a little enlarged which she assumed was the result of her earlier problems. She said that whatever problems Becky had had at birth had apparently corrected themselves. She advised us to return in one year for another checkup.

Then I asked her about Becky's motor development. She was over a year old and still couldn't sit up or crawl. I pointed out how stiff her legs were and how she stood on tiptoe when I stood her up. I explained that I had asked our family doctor about this and that he had told me that many children walk on their tiptoes when they are first learning to walk. She said, "I don't deal with legs, only with hearts, but if you are concerned about this, why don't you make an appointment with pediatric neurology? They are the ones who would deal with that sort of thing." She assumed that we could return the following week for such an appointment. She went out to the desk and said to the receptionist, "Please make an appointment for Mrs. Burke with pediatric neurology for next week." The receptionist laughed and said that the earliest possible appointment available would be in about eight weeks, so we took the earliest possible appointment.

From the vantage point of several years later, I am utterly unable to believe that the cardiologist did not know, or at least suspect what the problem was. I guess she didn't see any point in telling me that it was indeed an indication of a serious problem. By saying what she did, she avoided all discussion. It was frustrating for me to have to wait for an answer to that fearsome question, what is wrong? I think now that it is so painful to be the bearer of such dreadful news (that a child may have a permanent handicapping condition) that physicians avoid any discussions of this sort whenever possible.

When we returned to the pediatric neurology clinic several weeks later, we went through many of the same experiences, but this time we were prepared to stay all day. When the neurologist finally came in late in the afternoon, he simply pushed on Becky's feet, said "Ummm hummmm," and walked out into the hall and said to the nurse, "Cancel the EEG and send her to physical therapy." As he walked away down the hall, I called to him, "Wait, please tell me, will my daughter be all right? Will she ever walk? What is wrong with her?" He turned sideways and said, "Oh, it will take a while and may involve some night splints or some braces, but she'll walk someday." And off he went. I was just too shocked and exhausted to chase him again and press for more information.

For a while I was angry about the way he had treated me but now I think that maybe he felt very badly about having to make such a diagnosis. Becky was a pretty baby with golden curls and big blue eyes. She was already talking some at nineteen months and was very charming. It must be hard to tell the parent of such a pretty baby that her child will be faced with a permanent handicap.

I looked at the charge sheet the nurse handed me to take to the insurance office. In the space for diagnosis it read "spastic diplegia." When I got home, I called a friend who worked in a medical library and asked him to look up those two dreadful words. He reported back that they appeared under cerebral palsy and implied involvement on both sides of the body.

Well, we went to physical therapy, and the therapist was not very reassuring either. The first thing she said was, "Oh, she's so little!" I thought she must not have had much experience with babies. They usually are little. She showed me some passive stretching exercises to do with Becky's legs and finished with a warning that "these kids try to use their handicap as an excuse and can be really difficult if you don't really watch them." At that point I should have left her company for good but I didn't know where else to turn for help, so I came back a few more times. Things just went downhill, though. One of the next suggestions she made was for us to get Becky a tricycle. Now remember this child was under two years of age at the time and couldn't even sit up. Well, we got one. Getting Becky on it was not too bad because she could hold on to the handle bars, but there was no way she could use the pedals. Her stiff legs just slipped off, and she got tighter and tighter the more she tried to control them. That was the end of our association with that therapist.

We moved to Chapel Hill, North Carolina, a short time later, and I immediately got an appointment with a physician in family practice. I explained to him about Becky and asked him to refer us to the hospital at the University of North Carolina. He did and we went there a week later.

Here we found a wonderful difference in the scene. The neurologist was friendly and explained everything to me as he examined

Becky. He called in a physical therapist, and when she came into the room, we met the person who started us on the road to positive and constructive action to cope with our problems. She introduced herself as Carolyn Heriza and then began to play what appeared to be little games with Becky down on the floor. I recognized the test as one which tested cognitive and motor abilities in young children. She explained what she was doing and talked to Becky like one would to any three year old. When she finished examining her, she told me of a couple of options we would have for treatment and said, "I'd really like to work with her." Those words were like music to me. By that time Becky was noticeably different from a normal child in her motor abilities. She could crawl and sit alone and was talking very well, but it was very noticeable that she could not walk. This had made many people shy away from her. It seems that many people get sort of a squeamish look on their face when they see a handicapped child and they surely don't want to work with them. To find someone who "wanted to work with her" seemed so delightful that I couldn't wait for her to begin.

As time went on, Carolyn gave me books to read and other information and the emotional support I needed to feel assured and positive about Becky's handicap and her future.

When Becky was approaching four years old, I asked Carolyn and Dr. Swisher, her neurologist, what they thought about nursery school for her. I felt that she could benefit from an educational experience, and I wanted her to have social experiences with her peers. They told me that they felt that she should go to school with normal children because all her abilities were normal except for walking. They said that they would be glad to serve as consultants to any program that she got into.

Carolyn called someone she knew who worked for a child development center in Chapel Hill and asked him if they would consider taking a physically handicapped child. He told her he would ask at the next staff meeting and let her know. The answer came back that they would consider it.

I submitted an application to the center and received a form letter saying that Becky could come to their summer program. I had indicated on the application that she had cerebral palsy and could not walk, but I thought that maybe they would not read that part. I called them and it turned out they hadn't. They seemed rather doubtful, but they agreed to let me bring her over to the center so they could see what she could do. These so-called experts asked me questions like "If you talk to her can she understand you?" and "Has her disease run its course?" when we talked on the phone, so I knew we were going to be pioneers.

I didn't coach Becky before we went to the center, but she seemed to realize that she was on trial and was at her best that afternoon. She crawled all around the room and got into and out of the little chairs with ease, colored and drew, talked and talked, told stories, asked questions, and was very charming.

They said she could come to the summer program and see how it worked out. It went well and she was allowed to come to school in the fall. The center is affiliated with an elementary school and at that time had four, five, and six year olds together in groups in an open classroom setting.

Things seemed to go well during the year. When I went in for my conference with Becky's teacher, she told me that Becky was doing well. There were a few times when things happened that made me a little doubtful. One time the teacher called me to tell me that Becky had fallen and hurt herself a little. It was a very minor incident and I doubted if the parents of normal children received phone calls over such trivia.

When the time came for my spring conference with the teacher, I was amazed at what took place. The teacher and another staff member ushered me into a private office for our conference instead of holding it out in the open classroom as usual. I was immediately alerted that something was up; but what, I wondered.

The teacher began by saying "I am going to tell you something and leave one word out. You fill in the blank if you can think of a good word." Then she said, "The _____ of having Becky in the classroom has worn off for the children. I don't know if you'd call it novelty or what, but at first the kids were anxious to help Becky and be with her. Now they just run over her and leave her behind." The other staff member went on to say that they did not think that I should apply to have Becky enrolled at the center for kindergarten in the fall.

At that time our school system was phasing in public kindergarten and each school had a lottery to see which of the children who applied could go to public kindergarten. The kindergarten program at the center was part of the public school system and therefore had a lottery, too, but they were asking me not to put Becky's name in. I was shocked but I didn't say much. I was unable to collect my thoughts at first, so I just promised to think about it and let them know my decision.

I called a friend and talked to her about what they'd said and she encouraged me to call some other people who were interested in the needs of handicapped children. I did this and also checked with some private kindergartens. I found out that most of them were doubtful about accepting Becky and did not have ground level facilities where she could get around easily. (They were mostly in church basements, etc.) There seemed to be nowhere for Becky to go.

I also called the supervisor of elementary education for our school system and told her about what they had told me at the school. Her reply was, "Well, they are the professionals. Aren't you going to accept their professional judgment about what is best for Becky?" I said I was not going to give up yet. Then I asked if I could observe the classroom for a few days to see if I thought Becky was inappropriately placed there.

I observed for a whole week of school and found that Becky had many friends and some enemies just like everybody else. She seemed to handle the academic program as well as any of the other four year olds there. After a few days of observing, I was approached by the educational director of the center who said she was sorry to hear that there had been a misunderstanding. Now, I knew there had been no misunderstanding. What had actually happened was that word had gotten around that I was calling everyone in town and talking about how my daughter had been denied a chance at a public school education because of her handicap. This had been brought to the attention of people who were embarrassed by it, and the teachers were informed that there had been a misunderstanding. I applied for the lottery and Becky got into kindergarten where she had a great year with a superb teacher.

This was one of the few times that I used strong tactics to get Becky what she needed. Usually a more conciliatory approach is better. I recommend using aggressive methods only when there is no other alternative. A parent must protect a child's best interests and sometimes this requires one to be unpleasant. I think that most of the time when someone is not doing what the parent feels is best for his child, it is because the professionals do not see the situation in all of its aspects. They take a narrow view that includes their own fears and prejudices. If at all possible, a parent should try to give professionals as much information as they need to see the child's whole situation. One of the most important responsibilities that the parents of a handicapped child have is this exchange of information with professionals. It is in this process of information exchange that many difficulties occur. Emotions enter into the process and, as mentioned earlier, the crisis time of diagnosis is often confounded by the emotions of professionals who must deliver the bad news. Parents' ability to receive information from professionals and give information to them is also impaired by the overwhelming emotions surrounding the presence of a handicapping condition in their child. For example, when I found out that the name of our enemy was cerebral palsy, I felt such pain as the images of those poster children flashed through my mind that I couldn't see or hear anything in the room around me. From the professional's point of view, although the term is not incorrect in Becky's case, cerebral palsy is an imprecise umbrella term for any motor impairment caused by brain damage from any cause and they don't like to use the term for that reason. These two different reactions to the same term further illustrate the difficulties involved in the parent-professional communication process. After the initial shock, I was glad to have a name to tell myself and for all the others to whom we had to explain it; but the doctor didn't give it to me, I had to find it in a book.

If professionals can remember that their emotions may interfere with their communication and with the parents' ability to receive communication, they can be prepared to deal with these situations more adequately.

When Becky was five years old, her physical therapist moved away to another state and we were transferred to another therapist. Jan Wilson has continued and expanded the important influence that physical therapists have had in our lives. Jan is a professional who gives information readily and clearly and who listens to what parents are saying. She has learned to include parents in all aspects of the planning and implementation of the child's physical therapy. She is also one who gives parents the emotional support they so desperately need.

We are so fortunate to have had the opportunity to work with some fine professional people while coping with cerebral palsy and its frustrating consequences. While I am doling out praise, I must include Becky's first-grade teacher, the classroom aides in her kindergarten and first grade, and the principal of her elementary school. They have all made it possible for Becky to have an almost normal school experience with all its attendant challenges and joys.

Becky is now about to enter second grade in a regular elementary school classroom. She still can't walk unassisted, but she is making steady progress, and she can't wait to walk into school on her first day in her new shoes.

The Helsels

Dr. Elsie Helsel

The Helsel family is comprised of Elsie, Bob, Bill, Robin, and Marge. Robin is now thirty years old and is mentally retarded, cerebral palsied, and epileptic.

Elsie is an associate professor and coordinator of Special Education at Ohio University. In the late sixties and early seventies, she worked in Washington, D.C., as a lobbyist. She has been active in program development for United Cerebral Palsy and for the American Association on Mental Deficiency.

Bob just retired from the chairmanship of the Math Department at Ohio University. In the late fifties and early sixties, he worked diligently first for the Association for Retarded Children and then for United Cerebral Palsy. He continues to counsel handicapped students at the university.

Bill, three years Robin's senior, received a master's degree in special education and is now teaching educable mentally retarded students at the high school level.

Marge, seven years Robin's junior, is now a teaching assistant in special education at Ohio University and is putting the courses on computer-assisted instruction.

The Helsels'
Story of Robin

Elsie's Perspective

Saturday Night

Dearest Mother and Dad,

I wish I didn't have to write this—you have worries enough now. But we may as well all know the facts and then meet each day's problems as they come. We can still hope, too, and those who can, can pray. Somehow little Robin's brain has undergone injury—whether through disease, degeneration, or developmental accident, the doctors can't say. Nor can they give any very encouraging prognosis. They think the impairment may not be progressive, and they also think it is partial (i.e., he will learn to walk eventually), and there is still hope that he may develop sufficiently to fall into the normal bracket in intelligence. If during the next year or so the impairment remains the same, then he will probably continue to develop according to a normal pattern but with this much retardation. No one knows how much brain tissue is necessary for normal development, and certainly no one uses all of the intelligence he has. Everything else seems to be normal, and he is in perfect health except for his adenoids which must be removed.

Robin and I went into the hospital last Monday night. I stayed with him the whole time. Here at Children's they prefer that the mothers stay, and they have lovely rooms, lounges, and dining rooms to take care of guests. Tuesday morning resident doctors and interns performed routine lab analyses and many examinations. Tuesday afternoon Robin had X rays. Wednesday morning they did a spinal tap for examination of the spinal fluid. From then on, Robin felt bad. A neuropsychiatrist checked him Wednesday afternoon. I would not put too much faith in his prognosis (which was not good) because Robin screamed the whole time and didn't respond to his simple tests. This was the weakest part of the examination and, in one respect, the most important. Thursday morning Robin went into surgery for an anesthetic and the removal of all the cerebrospinal fluid and its replacement by air so that an aeroencephalogram could be made. A Mayo-trained surgeon did this job—he was the only one to take time to explain what he was doing and why. Also, he warned me that there was a certain amount of danger in the operation, and he wanted me to know about it before he did it. Since this was just like any other operation, Robin was and still is quite sick. We must give him plenty of fluids and keep him quiet and resting for a week. This was the part of the examination that showed the unusual brain condition. All of these tests and the specialists' opinions will be sent on to Hopkins when we go. As soon as Robin recovers from the shock of this hospitalization, we shall write Johns Hopkins and ask when we can come. Dr. Baxter thinks it would be best to wait for summer. Then we could get some picture of change if there is any.

My fingers feel like lead and my heart, too. This is the hardest time because people keep calling and dropping in. When we get through this, we plan to ask our friends not to talk with us about it. We shall attempt to set up as normal a home atmosphere as we can because that will give Robin the best chance that is possible to develop. No matter what lies ahead, we shall love him and try to keep him as healthy and happy as we can. Then we can always hope.

Don't feel too sorry for us. Life has been very good to us and if we can't rise to meet this problem, then who can? This is a real test of our long period of training, yet we have much to learn of humility and everything to learn about faith. Robin may bring some fine things into our home.

Love to you both,

Elsie

P.S. Robin and I came home Friday night—I have been too exhausted to write. Now that we are home, Robin is much happier. He didn't like the hospital and, as usual, someone was always coming in for something and waking him up.

That letter was written thirty years ago. As I sit here at breakfast with my thirty-year-old cerebral palsied, mentally retarded, epileptic son, I still recall with anguish that week when my world collapsed. What I could not know at that time was that as a consequence of this tragedy, all of the events and experiences that would bring meaning, direction, and purpose to my life were about to begin.

I remember vividly the details of how I found out that Robin was seriously impaired. Robin was a second child, and from the time he was six months old, I had been questioning my pediatrician concerning his lagging development. For about a year, the pediatrician had been turning aside my questions and delaying any unusual procedures. Finally he agreed to a diagnostic work up at Children's Hospital. When the orderly brought Robin back from one of the procedures, a pneumoencephalogram, he inadvertently left Robin's hospital charts in the crib. I picked them up and read, "Entering diagnosis: Mental Deficiency." Before being discovered, I had read all of the reports. Soon, however, a harried nurse entered and snatched the charts from my hands with a stern admonition that I had no right to read their contents. In no time at all, a small group of white coats and dresses came bustling into the room to talk with me until my pediatrician could be summoned. When he came, they respectfully withdrew and left him with the awesome task of explaining why he had not leveled with me earlier concerning what mental deficiency was, what the prognosis was, and why I shouldn't rush off to Johns Hopkins where I had a pediatrician friend on staff. The only thing I really remember from that encounter is a garbled explanation of mental deficiency and the doctor saying, "We can't all march in the parade!"

To his credit, he did not recommend institutionalization or some other unusual disposition. He did advise me to take Robin home, love him, and treat him as a normal child, providing as normal a home life for him as possible. I packed up my baby and my hopes and dreams for him and tried to do just that. The discharge diagnosis was mental deficiency at a profound level.

I began to read everything I could lay hands on about mental retardation. I found the Gesell Developmental Scales and quickly picked up the aberrant motor patterns and the other indicators of delayed development. I also contacted my friend at Johns Hopkins. I told her about my findings on the Gesell and suggested that Robin might be cerebral palsied. This seemed more acceptable to me than mental deficiency. In making my appointment with Johns Hopkins, I asked to be scheduled to see Dr. Winthrop Phelps who was the authority on cerebral palsy at that time. However, the doctors at Hopkins refused to schedule an appointment, stating that there were no indicators in the report from Children's Hospital that Robin might have cerebral palsy. It wasn't until four years later that we finally got to Dr. Phelps. He confirmed the diagnosis of cerebral palsy and asked why the child had not been referred to him earlier.

Our story is not atypical—lots of parents have told me similar ones. Yet it has something to say to professionals concerned with the diagnosis and assessment of multiply handicapped children today— listen to the parents. They are frequently giving you the diagnosis.

Tears still come to my eyes as I look at this handsome, blue-eyed, blond son of mine and think what he might have become had not something damaged his brain. I can rationalize that his life has had tremendous significance through his influence on our family, but the hurt is still there. Certainly he has changed our lives and helped make us into a family that has contributed significantly to the whole movement affecting severely and multiply handicapped individuals.

By the time Robin was born, my life style and career plans were fairly well set. I had completed my Ph.D. in genetics and was playing out the role of faculty wife and mother. Vaguely, at some undetermined point in the future, I planned to return to the university and continue my research on chromosome mapping. To be honest and blunt, I was smug, self-centered, and an intellectual snob. Robin's birth and the problems attendant to trying to find services and adequate care for him abruptly changed the pattern of my life, my attitudes, and my plans for the future. Suddenly I was thrust into a totally different world with people from all levels of society. We had common problems and our children had common service needs. Through working together, we learned to know and appreciate people for what they were and not for their professional, financial, or social status. My attitudes changed not only toward people with handicapped children but toward all people with problems. Now I knew what it meant to be stared at, shunned, avoided. People became embarrassed when we brought Robin out in public or when we explained his condition— especially when they learned that he wasn't going to grow out of it or recover from it.

In the neighborhood where Robin was born and his problems were known, we had no difficulty with acceptance. Our neighbors learned about mental retardation and cerebral palsy along with us. They helped with our door-to-door campaigns and our projects to get services for Robin. However, when we moved to a more sophisticated, more affluent neighborhood, the problems of explaining and acceptance had to be faced anew. Our teen-age daughter asked if we could keep Robin in the house because she really didn't know how to explain his condition to her new friends. Our neighbors raised their eyebrows when the school bus for retarded children pulled up at our door. An interesting event came to our rescue, however. The patrol-car police in our neighborhood had spotted Robin laboriously plod-ding around the block with his quad canes. They stopped to ask him where he lived and Robin, who has no speech, pointed out his house. The policemen wanted to know if it was "safe" for Robin with such an obvious disability to be out alone walking around the block. "What if a child or dog should topple him over? What if he should get out into the street and get hit by a car?" After getting reassurances from us that Robin could manage very well, the policemen left but sent the fire of-ficer. He wanted to know the location of Robin's room and our plans for fire evacuation for him. He also asked permission (apologetically) to put a small decal on our window so, in the event of fire, the fire-men would know there was an invalid in the house. He told us it was difficult for them to find handicapped and elderly individuals in the community because most people did not want their neighbors to know about any incapacities their family members might have. When we suggested a PR campaign to explain the obvious advantages of such a service, he asked if we would be willing to let them take some pictures of Robin for an article in the local paper. We agreed and a few days later, the fire chief, in full regalia, followed by the hook-and-ladder truck pulled up at our door. Pictures were taken of Robin with the firemen and published in the village paper. Overnight Robin be-came a celebrity, and there were no more questions about "What's the matter with your brother? Why can't he talk?"

In working to get services for Robin, I developed skills and know-ledge in a totally new field. This led me into a new career of program consulting, writing, lobbying in Washington, and eventually into an administrative and teaching position at Ohio University. Now at a time and an age when most people are thinking about retirement, I must make choices concerning which job opportunities to pursue. Robin has indeed brought directions, purpose, and meaning to my life. I have achieved a degree of personal fulfillment that I feel I would never have attained in my former career as a bench scientist. I have seen more of the world, had opportunities to meet saints and sages, been part of the glamorous Washington scene, and worked side by side with top people in our national government. I have been on the cutting edge of the action in the generation of legislation and programs for the handicapped. Best of all, I have had the opportunity to earn the respect of my peers and colleagues, and I have the intense satisfaction of leading my own son and daughter into professional ca-reers in working with the handicapped.

On the minus side, I have had to come to terms with the obvious fact that Robin was not going to make it intellectually or education-ally. Hardest of all, I have had to sit back and watch him slowly lose function over the years, slowly lose incentive to try, slowly become more and more frustrated and unhappy. Seizure problems have now come under partial control, but each episode is a reminder that the old basic problems are still there.

Despite all the services, the knowledge, the counseling, the emotional support, living with a problem for thirty years takes its toll. I get tired dragging Robin around, making all the special arrangements that must be made before I can go anywhere or do anything. I get tired lifting that heavy wheelchair in and out of the car. It would be nice just to be free to take off on a moment's notice and not have to plan ahead.

Professionals are constantly probing and asking questions concerning how Robin's constant presence and problems affect our marriage. Once again, there are pluses and minuses. I really don't believe any one factor in a marriage can be pinpointed as a strengthener or strainer. There are too many variables affecting a marriage for such a simplistic explanation. The temperament of the individuals; the physical, emotional, and financial strengths; the problem-solving and coping skills; the commitment people bring—just to mention a few factors—all have some bearing on the strain a handicapped child brings to a marriage. From my point of view, I feel Robin has added more strength than strain. At least my husband and I are still living together after thirty-seven years of marriage! For one thing, at those points in a marriage when you are contemplating divorce—intellectually, emotionally, or actually—the presence of a child such as Robin in the family is a major deterrent. The focus quickly changes from your own needs, wishes, desires to your responsibilities, commitment, and the needs of the child. Somehow this helps you work through the problem, and you find another way. I have never bought the argument that the presence of an adult person in a family, be he handicapped or not, is a disruptive factor. I feel society has lost a mooring with the breakdown of the extended family. Romantic twosomes are great for novels and certain periods of our lives. I do not see such a pattern as essential for a successful marriage. My husband and I will not have a footloose, carefree, romantic retirement life style, but we will have something else—we will have the opportunity to feel needed as long as Robin needs us.

Bob's Perspective

The following section is comprised of a conversation between Bob and his daughter, Marge. They discuss Bob's perspective of being Robin's father.

MARGE: When you first found out that Robin was mentally retarded or cerebral palsied, what kind of gut reaction did you have?

BOB: I didn't have a strong gut reaction. We realized when Robin was less than a year old that he didn't show the normal physical reactions and abilities. It is my impression that I accepted this, even the brain damage. Elsie didn't respond that way and dragged us around to various clinics and authorities for diagnoses and prognoses. I went along with that, but not because I was expecting to find some cure or some hopeful prognosis.

MARGE: So it sounds like you had a pretty realistic outlook towards it, or, at least, you felt you had.

BOB: At least I felt so at the time, and I still feel so, although I might have been more emotionally involved and uptight about it than I realized. But my impression is that I accepted it, and there it was.

MARGE: You couldn't do much else?

BOB: That's right.

MARGE: Do you remember some of the initial reactions of our grandparents? I guess the only grandparent around was Grandma Dressler. Were their reactions just like those of other people, as you told them about Robin? Can you remember anything about that?

BOB: Three of the grandparents were living then—my mother and Elsie's mother and father. I feel that, like Elsie, her parents weren't too accepting, and they hoped against hope that we would find something to cure Robin. As I recall, my mother was more accepting. But she was the kind of person who put her trust in God, and she didn't get too upset.

MARGE: Did that make it harder for you, having them have a real emotional reaction?

BOB: No, I don't think so. I think at times I was irritated by the attitudes of Elsie and her parents. To me, it looked like their desires to have a normal child and grandchild were clouding their thinking. This can be irritating, but it didn't affect my attitude towards Robin. He wasn't the one profoundly affected.

MARGE: So you don't really think that it was such a bad thing necessarily?

BOB: No.

MARGE: How about other people, like neighbors? I suppose when he was younger, there wasn't that much contact.

BOB: Robin was a very loving baby and young child. Our neighbors responded positively to him. I guess we were fortunate in that.

There were no instances of neighbors shunning Robin or being upset by him. Quite the contrary. It was a good experience, I would say, in that respect.

MARGE: So Robin's nice personality kind of helped out?

BOB: Yes, it did. He was nice to be around. He was good-natured and loving.

MARGE: How about my brother Bill and me? Did you see any early reactions in us? Were we pretty much not aware?

BOB: Within the family, I didn't notice any adverse reactions. Again, Robin's personality played an important part there. He was a member of the family, and he joined in, and you and Bill responded and accepted him. Now, how you felt about Robin when you related to your peers, I really don't know. I assume you had a certain amount of shame and guilt, but I didn't see this because this occurred in contacts outside the home, and I wasn't part of that. But inside the home, Robin was one of us, and was accepted and loved. And he responded to this. He joined in our love and concern mutually.

MARGE: He wasn't a disruptive influence, then?

BOB: Not internally. I do think that you and Bill probably had difficulties outside the home because of Robin, not necessarily because of anything that anyone said or did, but simply because you feared you would be criticized, ostracized, or made fun of because of a handicapped brother.

MARGE: How did you feel about the educational services he received and how the teachers reacted? You were in sort of an interesting situation in that you were involved in the parent organizations [A.R.C. & U.C.P.].

BOB: We were the beginners, the people who formed the first classes for such children and who struggled to gain the proper services for them. As far as the actual class experiences and the way I felt about them, the teachers, of course, had no previous experience or training, so they tended to teach as they would teach normal children. This irritated me because I felt there was nothing that such a child needs less than the three Rs. What they needed—what Robin needed—and what such children need is training that will enable them to get along to the best of their abilities. And there really isn't any need to do spelling or arithmetic. Although you could argue that they could use arithmetic—they should be able to make change and so on. But this wasn't what they were teaching. When I was in charge of the classes for retarded children, I wasn't happy with the teaching. But I didn't try to impose my views although I voiced them often enough. I don't know whether the situation has changed greatly or not. I think there is still probably the tendency to try to give these children too much formal education and too little of what they need to get along at home and in the street.

MARGE: So you think his education left a lot to be desired as far as meeting his needs?

BOB: That's right. And because of its formal character and his inability to respond in a manner acceptable to the teachers as far as learning to write, read, and so on, it was extremely frustrating for Robin. It was a bad experience for him. He rebelled against it because he couldn't measure up. As I said, it disturbed me because I felt this wasn't relevant to his future life and wasn't what was called for.

MARGE: What eventually happened?

BOB: He just wouldn't go to school anymore.

MARGE: At what age was this?

BOB: Oh, I don't know if I can give you the age.

MARGE: Just a rough estimate.

BOB: We had him in classes of one kind or another, I suppose, for a period of ten or more years. This would mean that when he finally rebelled to the extent that we stopped pressing him to go, he was perhaps sixteen years old, something like that. But he never had what I considered a satisfactory experience for him.

MARGE: You feel like other people were trying to say, "This is what he should do," and weren't looking at him as an individual and saying, "This is what he needs"?

BOB: Or, "This is what we hope to have him achieve." You're quite right. They never tried to measure his abilities and interests. They tried to impose preconceived notions about what people should learn in school. He didn't learn them and so he was unhappy, and the teachers, of course, weren't particularly happy with him.

MARGE: Do you feel this bad early experience with education has affected where he is now?

BOB: It's been a factor in his growing frustration. I mentioned that Robin was a very loving child who was enjoyed by, I think, all of the people who knew him. But his personality has changed over the years and reflects his growing frustration, and certainly his inability to do what was expected of him in a school situation was part of that frustration. I think it wouldn't be fair to blame it on the schools and say that that is why he is now a frustrated individual, but they added their bit.

MARGE: They didn't add the right bit or something? Robin's had a lot of illness—how has that affected you? I know it's upsetting for any parent to have a sick child. Did his illnesses place a special burden on you or did they help you in any way?

BOB: Well, it doesn't affect me anymore than the illnesses of my other children. A parent is sick when the child is sick. These things I suppose eventually leave their mark on the parents' health and well-being. But I don't feel that Robin's illnesses have been any more traumatic for me than the illnesses of my other two children, not as traumatic as Bill's illnesses.

MARGE: He was a lot sicker? Are your reactions toward Robin different now as opposed to when he was younger?

BOB: Well, I've mentioned that Robin's personality has undergone great changes as he matured and came to know his limitations and was frustrated by that. And in the same way, my reactions to Robin, my personal attitudes, have changed over the years. I think I enjoyed Robin very much when he was quite young and didn't feel as badly about his handicap as I do now. As I see his growing frustration, my sympathy and empathy for him increase, but at the same time, the manifestations of his frustration—tantrums and such things— cause my tolerance to wear thin. At least, the limit of my tolerance is approached. In other words, he's harder to live with now—much harder to live with.

At no time have I regarded Robin as a burden. I always felt and still feel that I'm fortunate to have a handicapped person in my family. It is through him that I've learned tolerance for other people of lesser abilities and different abilities. I know that my teaching has been deeply affected by him. I no longer judge a student on the basis of what he can do in mathematics. I try to look at him as a person. I think no less of an individual who can't do mathematics. I don't think less of a person because he lacks some physical ability, like high jumping seven feet. So, Robin's handicap has been a very constructive influence in my life.

MARGE: That's a nice thing I hear you saying—that he's broadened your awareness of individual differences or whatever you want to call it, and made you more accepting, you feel, of other people.

BOB: That's right. And I also realize through Robin that every individual has a contribution to make to the people around him. And Robin has certainly made contributions. Earlier, because of his loving nature, and more recently, as I became more fully aware of his frustrations. There is also another reaction to Robin that I might mention, which is highly personal. Probably no other member of the family has it. Since I enjoy getting out in the woods and roaming around, I often stop when I am out hiking to think of how much I wish that Robin could have such an experience. I suppose that my desire to keep in good physical condition and remain active is in part a reflection of his physical incapacity. I wish somehow I could do it for both of us—to see nature, love it, and enjoy it not only for myself but for Robin, too.

MARGE: It makes you sad that he can't share that? I know how important it is to you.

BOB: As I said, I think part of the importance is that because I am so aware of his incapacity, it is all the more important for me to enjoy it fully.

MARGE: But, knowing you, I don't think you have ever forced Robin to do things that he couldn't do just because you wanted him to share an experience with you. Do you have any feelings about this?

BOB: No, I think I've been a fairly reasonable father as far as not pushing Robin. Although in some things, I would have been stricter than the other people around him. I would have been inclined to make him tow the line a little more and behave in a more acceptable manner.

MARGE: So you think other family members were a little too lenient?

BOB: Yes. But I don't know that I would have been right, and I am glad that I didn't insist because I could have been wrong. But I did feel that because of his handicap and because he was not the oldest member of the family, he probably was permitted to misbehave and show his anger and frustration more than he should have, more than was good for him, because he has a very low threshold as far as going into tantrums is concerned. This isn't to his benefit. But perhaps it is part of his condition, too.

MARGE: Returning to what you said about the increasing frustration that you feel he feels, are you worried about it?

BOB: I'm not worried. It's just that it moves me deeply, and I feel frustration in that I can't relieve his frustration, so my feelings about Robin and my attitudes toward him are certainly much different than they were when he was young. Simply, as he has changed, I have changed; not in a way that makes me less accepting. As I just mentioned, I feel more frustrated about Robin now than I ever did before.

MARGE: Can you tell me more about the frustration? Do you have concerns about where he is going to be and what he is doing right now? Or is it just sort of an aching, all-over feeling, not really specified?

BOB: It's a general condition. I just wish I could help him recapture the kind of attitudes that he displayed as a youngster. I wish I could relieve his frustration. I wish I could make him a happier person. But I don't know how to do this, and I don't know whether anyone can do it. It just bugs me; it is a constant thing.

You mentioned worrying about the future. I suppose this is the biggest worry that a parent of a severely handicapped child has—what happens when I die? And there is no answer to that. As far as I know, there is no way to provide properly for him in the eventuality—at least, I don't know of any.

MARGE: So you know it's there, but you're not sure of the steps and don't think there are any.

BOB: You can't amass enough capital to set up a private home for such a person. There just isn't an answer or a way to provide properly for such a child after your death.

MARGE: That's a real heavy thing to think, anyway. How would you summarize Robin's impact on you? You said some things about how he has opened up your awareness of other people and of your love of the outdoors and wanting to share that with him. Are there any other ways that Robin has had a direct influence on you?

BOB: I can't think of specifics. I'm convinced I'm a better person because of Robin's presence in the family. He made me into a better parent, a better teacher, a better person.

MARGE: How did he make you into a better parent?

BOB: Well, I learned a lot of tolerance, forbearance, love, and acceptance. These are qualities that make a good parent.

MARGE: So, all in all, you feel that Robin's being in the home has been a good experience for everyone involved?

BOB: Certainly. In some sense, every home should have a handicapped person in it just to heighten their awareness of the needs and limitations of other persons.

MARGE: Can you think of any special problems that Robin presents, has presented, or will present, to you?

BOB: Well, I would say in the past he didn't present any special problems with respect to limiting my life although I certainly put lots of time into a lot of activities for various groups trying to set up and maintain facilities for handicapped people. But he was a member of the family. We had other children, so taking care of Robin didn't place any special burden on us.

But it seems to me as I approach retirement age and would like lots of personal freedom, he will present a problem in limiting my ability to go where I want when I want. I'm not worried about this, but it is a fact. I don't know whether a solution will be found to give me the freedom that I would like to have or whether we'll just continue to be somewhat limited because of Robin. There are facilities opening up to take care of handicapped persons on a short-term or long-term basis which we might utilize. Such facilities would give us the freedom to travel or go on more hiking and backpacking trips. I am aware of the possible limitations on the freedom to leave the home.

MARGE: A freedom which most parents of normal children hopefully have when their children are out of the nest.

BOB: Or if they aren't out of the nest, they are at least old enough so that the parents can say to them, "Take care of yourselves; I'll see you next month!" But with Robin, we can't do that.

MARGE: You said that *now* you're wondering about there being some limitations on your freedom, but when he was growing up, you didn't.

BOB: Oh, I didn't feel this because I didn't have any freedom to speak of. I had a job to go to every day, and there were the other children, so he didn't place any particular restrictions on me. But now I do know that it is a possibility.

MARGE: But it sounds like you're beginning to think through some solutions like maybe a group home.

BOB: I'm sure that whatever develops, it will be satisfactory for all concerned.

MARGE: But it's a valid point that it's a situation that should be dealt with.

Bill's Perspective

While growing up, I remember my mother on several occasions saying that she had planned my brother Robin to be a companion for me, apparently feeling that his handicap prevented this from occurring. However, recalling childhood days, many fun-filled occasions which we shared together come to mind. At that time, I don't think I really thought of Robin as a handicapped person—we just naturally designed play activities in which we could participate together.

Our Columbus, Ohio, home had a play den area which was our domain. On many occasions we would construct elaborate forts, complete with labyrinth-like passages and secret gates. Robin could adeptly maneuver his way through all of these constructs; he especially enjoyed demolition procedures when it was time to re-design our surroundings.

Similarly, at our summer home in Pennsylvania, we would pass hours building sand castles and roads—I doing most of the building and he the tearing down. We also perfected wonderful sand "pies" and "paving cement"—recipes now lost to posterity. On one occasion we built a road through the adjacent woods, a project deemed foolhardy by our parents; yet in later years our rustic trail became a main thoroughfare when our family constructed a larger home nearby. We should now be rich if we had collected a nickel toll for each foot passenger traversing our thruway.

Robin has always demonstrated keen perception when addressing a problem situation. As a very young child, still unable to crawl, he perfected a unique rolling technique for locomotion. On the occasion of an adult social gathering at our home, he rolled upon the scene and proceeded from guest to guest, emptying all beverage bottles left on the floor.

On another occasion, he took the gun-cleaning rod used by my father to administer spankings to both him and me, bent it up like a pretzel, and carefully replaced it on the proper closet hook where it was discovered by Father the next time its use was desired. I, unjustly, was accused of the crime and duly punished. Perhaps my collabora-tion was assumed based on previous occasions when I had instructed Robin in such activities as dismantling his bed. I recall his being an able learner, needing only one demonstration to master this and similar tasks.

Robin's capacity for remembering things has always amazed me. As a child he would bury toys in the woods around our summer home and return to excavate them the next year, proceeding to the correct location without hesitation. Likewise, as an adult, one never men-tions something casually in his presence, assuming that it will either pass him by or be forgotten.

Although unable to speak, Robin has developed his own affective language system, consisting of self-created gestures and sounds. At times, he has stumped all of us in trying to figure out what he wants to say (we often resort to our own version of 20 questions). Despite speech limitations, Robin understands all of what he hears being said around him, including the points of subtle jokes and stories. On more than one occasion, he has surprised house guests by reacting to something they were saying which they apparently felt he would not understand or pay attention to.

Robin's favorite vice is drinking beer, which he acquired a taste for as a young child. I really don't know what his capacity is, but it is more than enough to put me under the table. At social occasions in our home, Robin can usually monitor himself and not overdo it; however, when he is angry and alone in the house, he has emptied the refrigerator, somehow managing to get the tops off of bottles (something we felt he couldn't do for himself). When asked if he drank all the beer, Robin put his finger to his lips and made a shushing sound.

The first significant change in my perception of Robin occurred when he became physically too large to be included in those family activities where before he had been carried or transported in his carriage. At our summer home, Robin dearly enjoyed going swimming in the nearby creek, but the rough terrain prohibited our carrying him there once he became a teen-ager. Father and Mother bought Robin a large plastic swimming pool which was set up next to our house. In it we enjoyed many a water battle—but it was somehow different from before. Similarly, Robin's participation in other family activities away from home lessened as he became older.

I have observed that adolescent children in many families tend to become very independent and ignore family activities, so I can't say that our family would have remained one in which many activities were shared if Robin had not been handicapped. Today Robin has his own interests as I have mine. It is easy to look upon his routinized life style and prescribe changes for his betterment. Still, I don't think his life is substantially less happy or satisfying than my own. Despite our different life styles, we share many common joys and frustrations.

Someone outside the family could easily look at my life pattern and infer causal relationships to the fact I grew up in a home with a handicapped person. Certainly there has been some influence, but it has been more indirect than direct. By this I mean that Robin and I share an interpersonal relationship based primarily upon personality and only secondarily upon physical circumstances. Living with Robin has made me more aware of and sensitive to persons with special needs—but we are all persons with special needs—each asking for attention and understanding. Conversely, Robin's presence has not meant that I am always at ease in the presence of handicapped persons or can always look upon them in a positive light without feeling distressed or disturbed.

Probably the most significant difference between my situation and that of a person not used to living with a handicapped person is that the situation is neither strange nor unusual to me. Because of this it is sometimes hard to remember the difference between my perspective and those of other persons. To this point, I recall my wife telling me how nervous she was the first times that she met Robin, not so much because of him, but because I was not providing her with information to help her relate to him. While handicapped persons, like ourselves, do not wish undue attention called to their situations, those persons unaccustomed to being with them may appreciate some guidance.

Marge's Perspective

As a young child, I cannot recall considering Robin to be retarded or in any way different from myself or the other members of my family. He was simply my brother—an affectionate presence during my early years and a welcome playmate during the summers my family spent at our somewhat isolated country home in Pennsylvania. I remember Robin as a willing guest at afternoon tea parties beside the small stream that ran through our property and evenings filled with giggling and pillow fights in the room he and I shared in our cottage.

When we returned to the city in the fall, I can recall accompanying my mother each morning to the rather grim-looking building where Robin was enrolled in a volunteer-run school for retarded children. Even then, I did not think of him as being different. In my mind, he was just going to school as I knew all children of his age did.

I cannot pinpoint exactly the time or the circumstance when I first became aware of Robin's handicaps. Several incidents come to mind, all of which occurred around the time I was eleven years old. One involved a trip to the shoe store where Robin was to be fitted for orthopedic shoes; another, a trip to the town near our country home for dinner at the YMCA. On both of these occasions, I can remember being acutely embarrassed by the ill-concealed stares our family received as we entered pushing Robin in his wheelchair. I was certain that everyone was looking at my brother with his obvious handicap and then wondering what was wrong with the rest of us. As a result of the feelings aroused in me by these occurrences, I began to refuse to go out to dinner or shopping with my family and took precautions to avoid being seen on the street or in the yard with Robin.

These avoidance procedures on my part were not taken without an accompanying sense of guilt. I knew that it was wrong for me to be ashamed of my brother. I loved Robin dearly and realized that the opinions (real or imagined) of others should have had no bearing on my relationship with him.

Looking back, I think I would have benefited from some counseling during this period. As an adult, I now realize that my reactions to Robin's handicaps were not unusual, but I certainly did not know this at the time. It would have helped me to be able to talk with an adult other than my mother or father about the feelings I was experiencing because I think it would be extremely difficult for any youngster to admit pointblank to her parents that she is embarrassed by her brother. I believe most children growing up in a society which places a great deal of emphasis on so-called normalcy come to a point when they are ashamed or even outright reject a disabled sibling. It is at this time that they should be given a concise explanation of the disability (i.e., what it is, why it happened, the prognosis), be permitted the opportunity of exploring their feelings about their sibling and, if necessary, be given some guidance in problem-solving and coping skills to help them deal with their feelings in a constructive manner.

Following my period of avoidance, I entered a phase of false pretenses. I forced myself to appear in public with him—but only if I felt I looked my very best (freshly washed hair, make-up, a snazzy outfit, etc.). My specious reasoning was that if people were going to stare, they weren't going to find anything wrong with me. Also, though I am reluctant to admit such a selfish thought, I suppose I wanted to encourage people to think along the lines of "Oh, dear, look at that sweet young girl pushing her poor crippled brother around. What a wonderful child she must be." This period extended into my college years, at which time several events occurred that led to an abrupt change of attitude on my part.

Robin has periodically undergone hospitalization following seizure episodes which left him in a comatose state. I recall vividly my sense of dismay the first time I awoke in the morning to find my brother's room empty and no sign of him anywhere in the house. I remember rushing to my parents' bedroom to find them lying in bed fully clothed and my mother's tearful explanation that Robin had become ill during the night and had been taken to the hospital. Because I was too young at the times of his early hospitalizations to visit Robin, these episodes did not really have too much impact on me. Robin always came home after a few days, perhaps a bit less alert, a bit less his enthusiastic self; and our family life resumed its usual course. One day when I was a freshman in college, I drove out to my parents' house for a visit. I went into Robin's room to say hello only to find it once again empty and to hear my mother tell me that Robin was in a coma at the hospital. I remember the shock of the news and my sense of urgency to see my brother. I recall the agonizingly slow drive to the hospital, the walk down the long, forbidding corridor to his room. There my brother lay in bed, connected to all sorts of tubes and looking quite pale and helpless. My heart went out to him. I rushed over to the bed and picked up one of his hands. I felt that if I could only get him to give me some sign of recognition, he would recover. I stood by that bed and called "Bucky"—our pet name for him—over and over, praying that he would hear me and respond. After a seemingly interminable period of time, he finally did open his eyes and weakly squeezed my hand. I felt I had been given the best gift in the world. It really hit me hard then how much I did love Robin and how very precious he was to me just the way he was.

After the experience in the hospital, my parents encouraged me to become involved in several volunteer programs serving the developmentally disabled. Through programs at the local mental health center and a state institution for the mentally retarded, I began to come in contact with special educators and other individuals who genuinely accepted and cared for persons like my brother. These people taught me the value of viewing everyone, developmentally disabled or not, as unique individuals filled with potential and worth. Gradually, I found myself talking more about Robin to others, introducing him to my friends, taking him places. In short, I had finally learned to accept Robin for himself.

Having Robin as a member of our family caused me to undergo a great deal of introspection which led me to insights into certain aspects of my character that needed to be changed. My contact with him, coupled with some sound advice from my parents, also unquestionably influenced my decision to pursue a career in special education. I had originally intended to enter the field of chemistry, and indeed I completed a bachelor's degree in that area. However, something about my choice bothered me. I enjoyed the lab work and the excitement of scientific discovery, but something was missing. It wasn't until my father, during the course of one of our "What are you going to do with your life?" discussions, pinpointed the problem when he quoted the following statement made by the philosopher Kirkegaard: "The door to happiness opens outward." What this meant to me was that one could only find true happiness through serving others. The choice of a career then became obvious to me. What better way was there to serve others than to enter the field of special education where I could help people like my brother lead more fulfilling lives?

I do not mean to imply that life with Robin has been all goodness and light. I have seen the strain that the responsibility of his constant care has placed upon my parents. I worry about the increasing frequency of his seizures and about what would happen to him should my parents become unable to care for him. Robin, himself, like all brothers I suppose, can be truly aggravating. It makes me angry to see him try to weasel his way out of doing things that I know he is capable of doing. Just the other day, I was scolding him for not clearing his place at the table. I guess my sisterly bossing was too much for him. He pointed at me and angrily made the sign for hand-cuffs—his way of indicating that I should be put in jail.

All in all, though, I feel that Robin has brought much good into the lives of my family. He has taught us a great deal about acceptance, patience, individual worth, but most of all about love.

Pointers for Pros

Having shared how we feel about Robin and how we perceive his impact on our family, what can we say to other professionals from our experience that may give additional insights into the needs of families with handicapped children?

First, the old cliché of "parent counseling" must go. The needs far exceed those of parents and they certainly encompass a great deal more than counseling in the traditional sense. A handicapped person places stresses on the whole family, so the whole family needs support and help in understanding the handicapped child's condition, his needs, both present and projected, the extra demands his presence will place on the family. The entire family needs help with feelings. They need to know that it is all right to feel resentful, embarrassed, uncomfortable, inadequate. They also need to be told about the joy, the love, the challenge, and the opportunities for growth and fulfillment that such a situation can offer. As new children join the family, they particularly need help. The fact that they have been born into a family with a handicapped person will not automatically equip them with the facility to explain their sibling to peers or to accept their feelings without trauma. Much of what a family needs does not fall into the realm of counseling. They need information, skills, knowledge, management techniques, indivdual and group therapy. We would like to suggest a term to describe the services needed by a family as something like "family supportive services."

In keeping with some of the needs outlined above—and these are only a few of the needs families will have over a lifetime—professionals intervening with families should recognize early that they, too, are going to need help. The thought that one professional or one clinic or one service can supply all the support families need is absurd. Trying to assist a family to cope with problems of the magnitude, complexity, and duration presented by the birth and identification of a handicapped child will require a team effort. No one person has God-like powers to know what is best for a particular family, yet countless professionals assume this role. Above all what families do not need is the Professional BIA (Big I Am). They need professionals who are well qualified in their fields but who have humility and empathy in the face of a tragedy such as the birth of a handicapped child. Parents do not need to suffer put-downs at the hands of professionals. Over our lifetimes we have become more and more convinced that some professionals should not presume ever to counsel parents. Parents particularly do not need professionals who are off on their own ego trips. Professionals should be objective and not lay their own hang-ups or preconceived notions on the families they are trying to help.

Second, professionals dealing with families with handicapped children should constantly remind themselves that families are different. They come to this situation with all kinds of backgrounds and experiences, all kinds of coping skills, all kinds of strengths and weaknesses. Families are not *all* "guilt ridden," "overprotective," "unobjective." No pat answers, clichés, prescriptions, labels fit all families.

Third, professionals should be current in their knowledge. They should obviously keep up in their professional knowledge concerning handicapping conditions, but they should also be knowledgeable concerning services available in the community, legislation affecting the handicapped, rights of parents, attitudes towards handicapping conditions in the community, realities of the financial cost, and feasibility of service plans. For example, during the past few years, there has been a complete turnabout concerning institutionalization and placement in the least restrictive environment at the community level. There has also been a quiet revolution concerning the rights of the handicapped to services. Professionals, particularly those preparing young people in the professions, have a particular responsibility not only to be current in their knowledge of today but also to be aware of trends for tomorrow.

Last, but perhaps most important, professionals should accept parents as full-fledged members of the management team for their children. Parents have much to contribute from the moment a child's atypical development is suspected. They spend more time with the child, have more opportunity to observe the child, and are more sensitive to the nuances of his condition. They also have lifelong responsibility for an impaired child. The laws and courts are mandating their involvement with the programming of their children.

We hope our experiences can contribute something to the professionals of the future who will touch the lives of new parents of handicapped children, helping them to find the joy mixed with the sadness, the hope mixed with the despair, the opportunities mixed with the disappointments.

Pearl Buck (1950) said it best so long ago:

Parents may find comfort, I say, in knowing that their children are not useless, but that their lives, limited as they are, are of great potential value to the human race. We learn as much from illness as from health, from handicap as from advantage—and indeed perhaps more. Not out of fullness has the human soul always reached its highest, but often out of deprivation. This is not to say that sorrow is better than happiness, illness than health, poverty than richness. Had I been given the choice, I would have a thousand times over chosen to have had my child sound and whole, a normal woman today, living a woman's life. I miss eternally the person she cannot be. I am not resigned and never will be. Resignation is something still and dead, an inactive acceptance that bears no fruit. On the contrary, I rebel against the unknown fate that fell upon her somewhere and stopped her growth. Such things ought not to be and because it has happened to me and because I know what this sorrow is I devote myself and my child to the work of doing all we can to prevent such suffering for others.

References

Buck, P. S. *The child who never grew.* New York: The John Day Co., 1950.

H. Rutherford Turnbull III

A lawyer who specializes in mental health and mental retardation law, among other fields, Rud Turnbull is on the faculty of The Institute of Government, University of North Carolina at Chapel Hill. He is active in local, state, and national consumer and professional organizations, is counsel for state and local mental health and retardation agencies in North Carolina, and has written extensively as a professional and a parent on legal issues affecting retarded citizens. His son, Jay, and his wife, Ann, are Rud's principal teachers about mental retardation.

Jay's Story

In many respects, nothing in my life had prepared me for Jay; in others, everything had. Jay was born on a glorious, bright, warm Baltimore day in May 1967. His delivery at Johns Hopkins was almost unexceptional—he was a breech baby and our obstetrician was late in arriving. From that point on, however, the unexceptional was the exception.

It's Better for You Not to Know

One of the first things I noticed about Jay was that he had a large, egg-shaped lump on the top of his head where most babies have a concave impression; in photographs at home, it is so noticeable that it is remarkable to recall now that nobody seemed to pay it much heed. Another early warning sign was his plain dullness—not that he wasn't a beautiful child with an abundance of blond curls; it is just that he didn't turn over, move about, push himself up on his elbows, or do the other things that my friends' children of his age had done. His pediatrician, now the head of the department of pediatrics at a large eastern state school of medicine, seemed to poo-pah my concerns; on measuring the circumference of Jay's head, he simply said Jay was within the high range of normalcy and a bit slow. When my ex-wife tearfully cross-examined him, giving ample display of our anxieties, his responses became even vaguer.

Were it not for Jay's having a hernia in the first year of his life, we might have waited far longer to have our suspicions confirmed that "something" wasn't within the high range of normalcy but was beyond the pale. Upon detecting the rupture, Jay's pediatrician admitted Jay to Hopkins for what ordinarily would have been a fairly simple operation, but it turned out to be rather more than that. The Hopkins surgeon gave Jay a thorough examination the day before the scheduled operation and immediately called off the surgery, explaining to me on the telephone that Jay's retina was unusually flat and that he wanted a neurologist to look at him. Later that week, after the pediatrician, surgeon, and neurologist had examined Jay, I learned that they wanted to do more tests before making a decision on his surgery.

My antennae were up—I was seeing danger signals in every phrase the doctors uttered. My questions—"Can't you be more specific? Have you had cases like this before? Why is the neurologist involved? Is something wrong with his eyes?"—went unanswered. I was told, "We can't say yet; we're still checking things (not him!) out."

On one of my frequent visits to the hospital to see Jay—his curls shaved off his head (they are in an envelope in our safe deposit box, remnants of our age of innocence), in a crib next to a child whose chart read "Nothing by mouth or intravenously" and whose head was far larger than Jay's—I saw a nurse I used to date and asked her to come see Jay with me. While we were visiting him, I picked up his chart and asked her to read the neurologist's report. After scanning it quickly, she said, "It's better for you not to know, Rud." And she left, suddenly saddened, taking with her my hopes for knowledge. The nurse in charge of the ward promptly appeared on the scene, admonishing me not to read the chart: "Jay's doing fine, Mr. Turnbull." Of course, he was: no worse and no better than at home. The point is, I wasn't doing fine at all.

A day or two later, still ignorant and waiting for the neurologist to undertake some minor surgical procedure, we waited and waited and waited for him to come to see us before the surgery. When at last he appeared, I turned all my anger and ignorance on him: "Before you so much as lay a hand, much less a scalpel on Jay, I want to know, I demand to know, what the hell's going on! And where have you been all this time!"

"Saving a life down the hall—and you've got the right to be angry, Mr. Turnbull. Let's talk."

Were it not for Dr. Neal Aronson, the neurologist who leveled with me, the entire staff of Johns Hopkins Hospital might have kept me in eternal ignorance. Simply, deliberately, humbly, and patiently, he explained all: Jay's flat retina, the little egg on his head, his slowness, and his "high range of normalcy" were signs of either macrocephaly or hydrocephaly. Jay, I heard him say, was retarded and very seriously so, although the exact degree was hard to pinpoint at his early age and would be hard to fix for several years. He ran a serious risk of surgery for the hernia. To better evaluate the risk, the doctors needed to do an exploratory—that is, look at his brain, making a very small incision, maybe blow air around his brain, or put fluid in and take pictures, nothing unusual or unusually risky. He let me know so gently that I felt not the pain of the future but absolution, the soft vanishing of my present and past anxiety.

*   *   *   *   *

In a remarkable gesture to all the fathers and mothers of all the Jays in the public schools, Congress has made it possible for parents to see their children's school records if the school receives federal assistance. "Accountability, parental rights to control children, school-home dialogue and teamwork, due process, misclassification"—these are the concepts underlying the Buckley-Pell Amendment. As a lawyer, I am convinced of the correctness of that legislation and of the need for similar legislation in the fields of health and mental health. As Jay's father, I quickly balance "It's better for you not to know" against a motto that I believed years before when I was an undergraduate student, and that Dr. Aronson believed and acted on: access is not only invaluable to parents and professionals, it is imperative as a course of decent conduct between people and as a weapon against charlantry, from which I have been largely spared (unlike other authors in this book).

*   *   *   *   *

Jay's surgery went well, his hernia was repaired successfully, and he came back home with the recommendation that he be put into a behavior program at the Kennedy Institute, an adjunct of Hopkins Hospital. Trusting and hopeful, we duly enrolled Jay and were obliged, as part of his program, to watch a professor of psychology try to get him to say "Aaah" in exchange for a spoonful of banana pudding. "We want to teach him to react to his environment, to control it," we were told. And that's all we were told, even after questioning. We saw failure after failure. In the name of what? Helping Jay? Collecting data?

Leaving aside (if one can) the irreparable injury Jay's repeated failures had on my ex-wife and me, and not daring to calculate the almost numberless times parents have had their children's deficiencies so pointedly and callously highlighted by "helping professionals," I wonder, as a lawyer, whether the concern that we attorneys have with consent—and the professionals' growing concern with it—is sufficiently impressed on all of us. How many programs have children been enrolled in without their parents ever truly knowing the who, what, where, how, why, and how long of them? When did my trust turn to skepticism? When I first asked, "What's in it for Jay?" That simple question is not asked often enough. "Informed consent" troubles us all, and rightly it should. We don't have enough of it.

The Search

Gaps exist in Jay's story, at least as it is told here, but they stop in the years 1970 and 1971. In those years, for many reasons, not the least of which was Jay (still beautiful, still heartbreakingly retarded, still without programs of any benefit) I began the search—our own family Diaspora. When my ex-wife was hospitalized for treatment of emotional disturbance and determined not to come home until Jay was no longer there, I faced what I immediately recognized as a horribly cruel choice. Which of those whom I loved would I have to give up? Whose immediate future held more promise of habilitation? That one would consign the other to an institution. For reasons not necessary to be told, I chose to "place" Jay. At first it was easy—Cordelia, a huge, black woman who worked at the day-care center in Durham that Jay attended offered to take care of him. He lived with her in a home I saw only once, where he thrived until the always tearful, rending visits I made to the center. I made fewer and fewer visits as they became harder and harder for him and me. Both Cordelia and I knew that Jay's being with her would never be permanent, and I was constrained to begin my search for a school that would accept a nonverbal, nonambulatory, not toilet trained, almost three-year-old boy.

My search took me from Massachusetts to South Carolina, from expensive, pretty, and small institutions to large, dilapidated, reasonably priced, and overcrowded ones. I saw children whose very existence caused me to wonder (I balanced "Do not feed . . . " against my four years of daily religious regimen in a boys' Episcopal boarding school—"God's mysteries . . . ") and whose appearances were, at first, horrid to behold (a head on a tiny body, three times out of proportion to the body; an open spine on an infant whom the Sister cradled, affirming the right of that child to live and to live with love). Later I was repulsed as I saw patients in institution after institution sitting in butterfly chairs all day long, dressed in the same faded denim, in places that smelled of the same stale urine and disinfectant, on the same terrazzo floors, in wards where no partition separated beds from chairs from toilets with no seats from steel tubs for bathing. I asked myself why the state couldn't do something about these places.

I inspected almost thirty institutions in eight states in a period of three months, and all I could find for Jay was the "nonambulatory" ward of a state institution nearby (I vowed Jay would *never* go there) and the unclassified wards in two small Catholic schools. How was I to choose between the two? Surely by the people involved, since the facilities in one were pathetically overcrowded and the facilities in the other were old. It was my choice to make, and mine alone.

As fate would have it, I chose well and wisely. Sister Mary Howard's Pine Harbor School in Pascoag, Rhode Island, no longer exists physically. The diocese ran out of willing Sisters and sufficient funds, and the state association for retarded children and the state joined hands to condemn the school as unsafe. Yet it still does exist in Jay's life and my heart. It was there that Katie McCarthy and her family "adopted" Jay when they saw him in the Christmas play. It was at Pine Harbor that, in the most wrenching moment of my life, doing the act that was then and still remains the hardest of my life, I handed Jay to Katie, a teen-age volunteer and an utter stranger; crying, burbling, stammering, I managed only to say, "Take him, he's yours now." Jay's screams, and his look ("Again? You are leaving me again!") remain with me today, vivid, poignant, immediate.

Pine Harbor closed, and Sister Howard and Katie took Jay to Crystal Springs Nursery in Assonet, Massachusetts. There he made friends in the "classroom" with other children approximately his age, and, now able to stand and walk (I first saw him walk at Katie's, for she was the one who taught him to walk), he toddled after them as they left for their group home. "Would it be all right if he were transferred off campus to the community group home?" the administrators asked. "Oh, by all means," I replied. "It's an old house, but it's fixed up nicely, and there are two wonderful house parents there; are you sure you don't mind?" "Not as long as he can be with his friends and have a chance for love," I said.

Sue and Dom D'Antuono cared for Jay and his "brothers and sisters" for two years, until Ann (my new wife) and I brought him home. Now every night he begins his prayers with "God, bless Sue and Dom and Paul Taylor (his roommate, with bright brown eyes beneath an Afro) and Johnny Corkle and Elaine Loomis and Michele and Annie Raffle. . . ." He catalogues his love in his prayers; love learned in an institution.

Nowadays it is sometimes and in some places fashionable to posit that parents and their retarded children have inherent conflicts of interest; accordingly, it is argued, the state, in its duty to the children, should inquire into the decision of the parent to place the child out of the home. The method of intervention should be a due process hearing, conducted in court or before a quasi-judicial body, in which the parents and child (represented by counsel of the state's choice) can give evidence why placement in or out of the home is desirable, necessary, inevitable, or whatever.

The argument appeals to me as a lawyer. I am concerned about children, particularly retarded children. I have a fairly good idea about institutions (particularly state ones, since I work with staff in them and serve on the Human Rights Committee in one), and I have an abiding concern, common to most lawyers, with fair procedures as producing fair and acceptable results.

But when I look at myself as a parent, I shudder to think about my search: my family in disarray; my home declared unacceptable for Jay by one member of the family; temporary care being only temporary; many institutions clearly unpalatable by even the most desperate persons (until they become in extremis and accept what little is offered by the state); and, in, around, and throughout it all, Jay's love for me and mine for him, permeating, soaking in, making rational choices difficult and all the more agonizing. Due process for Jay? for my ex-wife? for me? in the circumstances I have just described? Always? No choice about the hearing on anyone's part except Jay's lawyer? (And what about the right to be represented? to choose one's own counsel?) The search is my family Diaspora. What role would the courts have had in my search? It's a question to ponder in these days of judicial activism in mental health. The lawyer and the parent in me speak to me in conflicting terms.

I have no such conflict, however, when I think of the inability and unwillingness of the states to comply with ICF/MR or JCAH accreditation standards. The public and private places I saw were, almost without exception, grim testimony to the urgent need to immediately upgrade the physical facilities and staff of institutions by whatever legal means are successful, including court action. Standards are minimal and necessary; they are never sufficient. Only good people can make institutions good.

You Can Always Come Home

It may seem incredible, but the day Ann and I took Jay from Sue and Dom and his friends was a sad day. "Once more, good friends, once more unto the breach," I silently recited—the breaching of bonds slowly and carefully nurtured by Jay and his friends.

It's not as though we had not been in touch with Jay, but telephone calls and a visit at Easter are poor substitutes for physical presence, for affectionate hugs, for quiet moments together on the couch.

What is more, Jay had been at school for just over three years. I had a rather poor idea about what I was getting into, and Ann speaks for herself in her chapter. But we were certain of one thing (and far less certain of many things now, three years later) and it was that Jay must come home. We knew about his classes, his friends, the field trips, about Sue's and Dom's mothers, who had welcomed Jay into their homes during holiday times.

But we were well fixed to help Jay. Both of us had served as president of the local association for retarded children. Both were on the board of directors of the sheltered workshop and the group home. We were advisors in a professional capacity to a host of state and local mental retardation agenices. Both of us had worked hard to get a primary class for the trainable mentally retarded started just in time for Jay to be a charter member. We served on the board of a statewide political action agency for handicapped children. Both of us could draw on a wealth of professionally qualified friends.

Sad to say, neither of us was fully prepared for some of what lay ahead. We learned, for example, that the community could be inhospitable. Some friends and colleagues recoiled when Jay went to shake their hands, as though he were contagious. Others were glad to have their children visit our house where there were always plenty of cookies and milk for neighborhood urchins in the afternoons. Bribery or positive reinforcement, call·it what you will, it didn't always work, and we had to tell the little ones' parents that friendship is a two-way street. And strangers, curious about this lad with the strange gait and large head, stared even as he, like "ordinary" kids, devoured his ice cream cone on a hot summer night on the town's main street.

The battles for Jay—those we fought when he was not in the picture as an immediate consumer for he was still in New England then—continued, only with greater force, for now we had an immediate stake in the outcomes. School boards, county commissions, mental health boards, and town recreation departments, at first reluctantly and then with some conviction, began to heed our pleas: take Jay's class out of the administration building and put it in a regular school; use surplus funds to keep the developmental center open; increase the range of programs for the mentally retarded; try to get the hot lunches to the kids at camp at least before 1:30 P.M.

Not all was bleak, by any means. Strangers became the dearest friends because they loved Jay, and he loved them back in his unquestioning, unbargaining, unrestrained way. Other people in town remain strangers to us, but Jay is greeted by many people when we take our Saturday outings downtown and in the mall, his circle of acquaintances and friends large and varied. Jay has changed the attitudes of people who can affect his life; he has given them an understanding and (what is more important) an appreciation of his needs.

A successful farmer in the north end of our county has learned to appreciate people like Jay. The ideologies and life styles of the people in the north end are markedly more conservative than those of people in the southern end, where the university is. This farmer laughs with us about the time I asked him to rent a home to the group home board for use by retarded women. "Will they shoot my cows?" he asked. I assured him they wouldn't shoot his cows or assault people, were able to care for themselves, and would earn taxable income at the workshop. Not persuaded, he investigated the group home board and later came to board meetings, listening intently as we talked about the program, house parents, residents, funding, etc. After one meeting, I asked him, "Mr. Pope, have you any questions?" He replied, "No, I don't think so. Come see me in two days, and you can pick up the lease."

Many months later and after innumerable alterations to his home and hullabalooing and indecisiveness by local and state licensing bureaus, Mr. Pope's house was ready for occupancy. Two nights before the first residents were to arrive, he attended the board meeting to say he had been talking to his friends in Cedar Grove (the community where the home is). Out of both curiosity and fear, someone on the board asked, "Have you heard any negative comments, any objections to the women?" He paused, smiled slowly, and said, with increasing firmness, "No, I haven't. I don't expect to. And I'd better not!"

Some mental retardation and mental health professionals view lawyers as adept Don Quixotes who tilt at windmills that the professionals have painstakingly created to serve the retarded (and, not wholly incidentally, themselves). Surely, that view is justified, but just as surely it is incomplete.

Litigation does indeed change social institutions by changing the *forms* (facilities, programs, bureaucracies) as well as the *norms* (the notion that the retarded are best put out of sight and mind) that underlie and support the institutions (law being one of them) that have so unfairly treated retarded citizens. In my work with state and local mental retardation professionals throughout the country, I am happy to say to them, both as a parent and a lawyer, that courts are coming to the rescue and are prodding other agencies of government, particularly the legislature, to mend its ways and amend its laws.

We are, however, at a crucial juncture in the rights-for-the-retarded movement, and finely attuned thoughtfulness must be the order of the day. Having established the retarded citizen's basic right to, for example, education and treatment, or against involuntary sterilization and peonage, lawyers and lawgivers move into the stage of monitoring compliance or noncompliance and of implementing the rights that are given universally but denied individually.

We must be careful, for example, to think hard about the intended and unintended consequence of forcing community facilities down the throats of a largely ignorant and sometimes hostile public. When we deinstitutionalize or mainstream, we must ask, Whom do we take from what and put where and how fast? Ann and I thought the answer was so easy and know now it is not.

Lawyers know that laws are unenforceable unless they have the weight of publc opinion behind them: prohibition and anti-abortion legislation bear witness to that fact. But lawyers also know that public attitudes can be shaped by law. The issue of which comes first—the law that changes an attitude or the attitude that makes the law practicable—is raised in the deinstitutionalization issue. It will take time to effect change so that all the Jays can always go home and stay home. But make the time brief, for there are many Jays and few ways now of bringing them all home.

Freedom to Choose

I have been fortunate in the past three years to have had the chance to put my professional training to work in the mental retardation profession. In these years, I have consulted with, advised, helped solve problems with, instructed, and written for a host of mental health and mental retardation agencies at the federal, state, and local levels. Because Jay and Ann have given me a good working knowledge about the deficiencies and capacities of mentally retarded people, I think my advice and counsel have been far more effective than that of a lawyer who lacks comparable personal experiences.

Several months ago, for example, the education committee of North Carolina's House of Representatives was debating the state's second effort at an equal educational opportunities act. During the course of debate, several legislators questioned the meaning of "appropriate education," a phrase used in both the federal and the proposed (and now enacted) state law. Directing their question to the Deputy Superintendent of Public Instruction, they inquired about the definition of "appropriate education" and were told, in effect, that he did not know what it means and that, in any event, the public schools could not afford to provide it to handicapped children and their teachers were not trained to give it. Astonished by this very blunt and negative reply, some of them turned to the sponsor of the bill, who turned to me for an answer.

"If your child is nonhandicapped," I began, "and can go to the bathroom by himself when you take him out to dinner and can return to your table having washed his hands and buttoned his trousers, you will think that an appropriate education for him does not consist of training him to do these small but very important acts. But if your son cannot do these things, it becomes very important to you and him for him to be taught to do them. His eye and hand coordination, his manual dexterity, and his physical strength become sources of real concern because you do not want to be embarrassed by him in public and you do not want him to embarrass himself. An appropriate education for one handicapped child, then, may consist of teaching him to button his trousers. Does that help?" Indeed it did. Everyone on that committee understood immediately the meaning of the term and its importance. Jay certainly helped me to be a better lawyer that day.

During the same session of the legislature, I was working with a committee consisting largely of lawyers on proposed (now enacted) legislation to enable mentally handicapped people to have limited guardianships. Many of the legislators and clerks of court who opposed the legislation could not understand the concept of limited guardianship. They assumed that a person was either wholly incompetent or not incompetent at all. How, they asked, can we know otherwise?

Using as examples Jay's adult retarded friends, I explained the gradations of capacity/incapacity that mental retardation professionals are accustomed to describing in their own language (i.e., profound, severe, moderate, mild), but I did so in words the legislators would understand.

"Suppose you know of an adult who wants to have a friend of the opposite sex. Suppose both are healthy and will want to have sexual relations. Neither wants children. Both also have limited understanding about money and how to make their way in the world. The girl has been instructed in alternative methods of contraception and wants to be sterilized. Should she be able to consent to that procedure on her own? Should she, on the other hand, be denied a guardian to help her make her way in the world?"

After my illustration, the committee members understood limited guardianship. Jay, Ann, friends in the group homes, friends at the sheltered workshop, and residents at the state institutions gave me answers to an otherwise difficult question.

Rights to education, appropriate placement, limited guardianship, and least restriction are concepts that have turned the world of professionals in mental retardation upside down, have caused us to ask questions and seek answers we did not think to ask a few years ago, and are the direct contribution of lawyers among others to the turmoil that surrounds the lives of retarded persons. If my experience in giving straight answers in simple terms to inquiring legislators who, if given the chance to do good or not and the proper instruction to know the difference, are more likely to do good than not, is typical of the contributions that other lawyers are making in courtrooms as well as in committee rooms, I believe lawyers are making significant contributions and that some turmoil and new questions are a small price to pay in exchange for the contributions. To probe, analyze, question, debate, and challenge are lawyers' functions. To provide answers is likewise a lawyer's function. My answers come from life with Jay, Ann, and our retarded friends.

It has not been possible to write this short piece without recalling enormous amounts of pain and an equal quantity of joy. The reader can only begin to appreciate what Jay and Ann have meant to me, personally and professionally. And I myself am just beginning to see the results of their contributions to my professional life as legislation and concept papers I have worked on for intensive and long periods of time survive the heat of public scrutiny.

At one point in my life, I knew none of the answers, much less the questions. At another, I was fairly sure of knowing many of the questions and at least a preponderance of the answers. But I am older now and, I hope, wiser. Jay, too, is older (and wiser?). As is true of Ann, so it is of me: I have learned that I still have much to learn. I am wary, then, of certainty and of advocates (in whatever role) who say they have not only all the questions but all the answers as well. Do they have available to them the central question and answer? Do they have Jay?

Do they understand, as Ann and I do, that mental retardation is not most accurately described as a condition but as a process? Jay's life has changed drastically several times in his brief ten years, and he himself has changed and will continue to change. Inflexibility and dialectics would not have helped him or others of us caught up in the process. Rather, freedom of choice in acquiring knowledge about Jay, in being informed about his placements, in having available alternative places for him to live, and in being able to obtain services that fit his abilities and disabilities as they exist at different times should be the moving factor in law reform in the area of mental retardation. If the law is to assist Jay and others like him appreciably, it will be because lawyers, lawgivers, and policy makers have given careful thought to what it will mean for retarded persons if they and their parents are given freedom of choice.

My present belief is that it is the function of law and those who make and affect it to create more choices for the retarded and their parents. I believe that many of the other authors in this book make the same argument in their own ways. If their stories are not atypical, and they certainly are credible, then we all cry out with the same message: let us choose, and give us more from which to choose. The felt need of our time has been the felt need of the past, the need for greater choice in responding to the evolving process of life with a retarded person. It is the function of law to respond by shaping the institutions of society so that freedom of choice can be increased for all the Jays of the nation.

Ann P. Turnbull

Ann Turnbull is on the faculty of the Division of Special Education at the University of North Carolina at Chapel Hill. She directs the mainstreaming project at the School of Education, is the director of graduate studies in the Special Education Division, and has published several books and articles on mainstreaming. She has taught retarded students in public schools and institutional settings and has worked as a regional consultant with special education teachers. She is an active member of local and state professional organizations.

Moving from Being a Professional to Being a Parent: A Startling Experience

I can vividly recall when I spoke three years ago to an interagency committee in a nearby community on the topic of deinstitutionalization. At the time I was a strong advocate for the quick return home of substantial numbers of mentally retarded persons from state institutions. I was interested in developing an educational program tailored to the needs of mentally retarded children and their families during the transition process from the institution to the community. I was in contact with the interagency committee to solicit the names of families who might be interested in involvement with such a program.

A social worker from a nearby institution attending the meeting reported that a ten-year-old female from the local community had been identified by institutional staff as having high probability for successful deinstitutionalization. Another member of the group stated that this child's parents had no interest in having her at home and that, in fact, they bitterly opposed the idea.

At that point, I remarked that it is difficult to understand that kind of parental response. Immediately a mother of a mentally retarded son flew to her feet and began berating me in front of the group. While shaking her finger in my face, she screamed, "Do you know what it is like to live with a mentally retarded child?" I felt both embarrassed and defensive. After trying to explain my comment, I responded (probably in somewhat of a self-righteous way), "No, I don't know what it is like, but in two weeks I will begin to find out. My husband and I will be bringing his mentally retarded son home from an institution." She smiled at me as if to say, "Are you ever in for it"; yet my confidence in approaching the new parental roles and responsibilities was unshaken. I had three degrees in special education with an emphasis in mental retardation, several years of teaching experience in public schools and a residential institution, and was on the university faculty with a joint appointment in a university-affiliated facility (an interdisciplinary program focusing on training university students in the diagnosis and treatment of developmental disorders and on providing services to handicapped children and their families) and the School of Education. Being with mentally retarded children was a way of life for me. I thought to myself, "Just wait. I will show you that it really is not all that difficult to be a parent."

When Rud, my husband, and I first became friends, we often talked about Jay or prepared "care packages" to send him. From the very beginning Jay was very much a part of our relationship. When we decided to get married, I insisted that we would bring Jay home. Rud was very pleased that our family would be together. So began Jay's deinstitutionalization.

Rud and I took a leisurely trip through New England and picked Jay up on our return at his school in Massachusetts. We were very happy to see him and filled with excitement and anticipation as we packed his things in the car. After a tearful good-bye to Sue and Dom D'Antuono, we started the trip back home to North Carolina. We stopped early on the first afternoon at a motel, so we could have a relaxing swim before dinner. As we approached the pool, Jay's temper tantrum started, and it did not end for a seeming eternity. He kicked and screamed and cried. Finally, when he calmed down, he got in the pool but would not budge from clenching the railing on the side. A girl much younger than Jay was swimming laps beside him. Her father, who was beaming with pride and clapping at her performance, turned to me and said, "Do you always have this much trouble with him?" I absolutely froze. I could not muster any kind of response. I wanted to shout, "Give me time. I've been his mother for less than a day." I choked my tears back and insisted that we go back to the room. Throughout the remainder of the trip home, the question kept echoing in my mind, "Do you always have this much trouble with him?"

Jay seemed happy with his new home. We spent the first days getting to know the girls next door and shopping for clothes. Jay was naturally very unsure about his new surroundings. He was unable to understand immediately what was happening. He had a new mother, a new home, a new school, and new friends. The only consistent contact in his life was his daddy, and Jay was determined not to let his daddy get out of sight. While on a shopping trip during that first week, Rud went to the bathroom while Jay and I were looking around in a department store. Jay panicked when his daddy left and started flailing around on the floor, screaming at the top of his lungs, "Daddy, Daddy, Daddy." It was the heartfelt plea of a child who had been left many times before. I ached for him, yet I ached for myself also when crowds of people started peering at us in my futile attempts to provide any comfort whatsoever. As the screams became louder and the crowds larger, I felt more and more helpless and inept. My image of being a model mother able to handle difficult situations was beginning to crumble.

For one who thought she knew, the last three years have, indeed, been a humbling experience. The twenty-four-hour reality test has standards far higher than any examination I ever took while earning my three degrees. In fact, the three degrees may have been more a hindrance than a help in meeting my new parental responsibilities. I had always been taught to be objective and to consider the facts of a situation. All of a sudden, I had an ache in my heart, a knot in my stomach, and tears welling in my eyes. It did not take long for it to dawn on me that the mother from the interagency meeting was right—I was in for a startling experience.

Jay was evaluated at the interdisciplinary clinic where I served as head of the Special Education Section. Suddenly, I was thrust into the parent role on my own professional territory. As I sat in the observation room watching him take test after test covering a five-hour period, I was shocked at how different it was to observe as a mother rather than as a special educator. College students were also observing in the same room I was in; it was standard practice at this clinic for students to observe. They were making remarks about Jay's language and motor skills and pointing out his particular deficiencies. I became incensed at how casually they made their comments. One made a comment about some developmental history she had read in the records. The privacy of Jay's past and of family business had been invaded by sheer strangers. Although I had known it was standard practice for students to have access to records, suddenly the issue of confidentiality took on new meaning when it was my family being exposed. After all the evaluations had been completed, several of my colleagues at the clinic went over the results with Rud and me. These colleagues were sensitive, supportive, and helpful. As I sat there receiving the information, rather than giving it (which was my usual role), I struggled to remain composed and in control. A glaring memory is the jolt I felt when Jay's IQ score was reported. It was much lower than previous tests had indicated. I could easily recite all the reasons that IQ tests are poor predictors of the future adjustment and employability of retarded adults, yet I still ached with the reality of Jay's severe handicap. At home that evening Rud and I wept from the tension of the day and our concern for Jay's future. I wondered how many parents had left a conference with me in my role as special educator and experienced the same reactions.

In Jay's first months home, I faced many of the emotional reactions that parents typically encounter immediately after the birth of a handicapped child. Almost all of my friends were professionals whose work related to the developmental problems of children. Many of them reacted to Jay as a patient or client, rather than as a child. I became very angry at their offhand remarks, and as a result, some of my closest friendships were abruptly ended. One friend commented, "I've never seen a child with such a big head." Another said, "Doesn't Jay remind you of an autistic child, the way he stares off in space?" How does a new mother respond to such a question? One unfortunate situation happened with one of my best friends who was also a special educator. Jay and I went to see her one Sunday afternoon to take a pie we had made for her to serve to her weekend company. Jay was beginning to feel more secure with me and happened to be in a delightful mood that afternoon. He told my friend and her husband about his school, sang some of his favorite songs, and listed the ingredients we had put into the pie. He laughed and played and enjoyed himself. I was so proud of him and could hardly wait to share with Rud the wonderful afternoon we had together. The next day my friend dropped by the office to thank me for the pie. She commented that her husband hardly said anything for the rest of the afternoon and evening after we left because he was so depressed after being with Jay. I was speechless. What did she mean? Jay had behaved perfectly at her house. Why was her husband depressed? I was unable to ask any questions or make any kind of response. She left my office, and a friendship was over. It seemed so unfair.

Yes, Jay is different. His developmental level is far below his chronological age. Will he spend the rest of his life depressing other people? Will we be able to find friends who can love and respect him for who he is? I was very confused at that point and felt alienated from many of my professional colleagues who were advising me to be objective and to remove myself from the emotion of the situation. In many encounters I was getting the message that they thought I was an obnoxious and hostile parent. I had been on the inside long enough to know what professionals think about parents who refuse their advice. I could remember having those feelings myself about parents. That's what really hurt. I felt both parental anger and sorrow over some of my own professional mistakes in previous interactions with parents.

One of the major hurdles in Jay's home adjustment was eliminating his wetting behavior. During Jay's first year at home, he went from being dry during the day to wetting his pants twelve to fifteen times per day. He also wet his bed several times during the night. We later found out that his incontinence was caused by medicine he was taking for his eyes, but we struggled with the problem for a four- to five-month period before we identified the cause. Every morning I would send eight to ten pairs of jeans and underwear to school with Jay; every afternoon he brought home a huge sack of urine-soaked clothes. Each morning his bedroom smelled of urine. Keeping up with the laundry alone was almost overwhelming. We were charting his wetting accidents at home, as his teachers were doing at school. No consistent pattern emerged. We started a program of taking him to the bathroom every twenty to thirty minutes, a program that resulted in very little success. He always seemed to wet during the intervals. His pediatrician started giving him kidney and urinary tests to pinpoint whether a medical problem existed. It was through her persistent and committed efforts that the connection between the incontinence and Jay's medications was established. A psychologist was also working with us and Jay's teachers on behavioral approaches. She spent an incredible amount of time reviewing charts and planning reasonable interventions. If all families of handicapped children could be fortunate enough to work with sensitive and competent professionals like Joanna Dalldorf and Carolyn Schroeder, how much easier parenting would be. Joanna and Carolyn worked with us on almost a daily basis through a very difficult period. They were supportive, flexible, and willing to try over and over again when their first efforts were unsuccessful.

We encountered our share of charlatans during that episode. While attending a conference, Rud and I were introduced to a psychologist who told us he was writing a book on managing the behavior of retarded children at home. We asked what suggestions he had for chronic incontinence as we described our problem. He flippantly replied that a problem of that nature could quickly be eliminated by feeding Jay a couple of sacks of pretzels every day. He explained that the salt would soak up the urine and the wetting would be eliminated. He was completely serious and smiled self-righteously as if he had the answer to all the world's problems. I suggested to him that he should include an obesity program in his book for the retarded children who ate all the pretzels. That type of easy answer to a very complex problem is the type of advice that creates mistrust and alienation between professionals and parents. Parents who spend their money on his book to try to find solutions to their day-to-day problems are headed down one more dead-end alley.

Another professional who worked at an institution for retarded individuals also had the solution to the night wetting problem. He recommended that we get up during the night every hour on the hour to see if Jay was wet or dry. If he was wet, he should be made to sit on the toilet and then to walk from his bed to the toilet twenty times. After changing his pajamas and the sheets on his bed, he should be allowed to go back to sleep only to be awakened again at the next hour. I laughed at his recommendation, and he quickly asked me how committed I was to eliminating the problem. The institutional staff, he reported, was willing to follow such a schedule. Among his other problems, he was failing to acknowledge that the third-shift institutional staff slept during the day. Imagine the havoc and frustration which would be created within a family by following such a regimen. As a professional I had feelings of bitterness that some of my fellow professionals were so insensitive and oblivious to their own lack of competence. The credentials and fancy titles were insufficient in masking the fact that they really did not know what to do, yet few of them were able to say, "I don't know."

Jay has had a profound influence on my professional life. Friends have often commented that Jay is very fortunate to have a mother who is a special educator. Really, it's just as true the other way around. There is no doubt that Jay has taught me far more than I have taught him. Some of the many lessons I have learned from being his mother are summarized below:

1. Professional behavior must be tempered by humility. It is impossible to have all the answers in regard to the diagnosis and treatment of problems associated with handicapping conditions. It was shocking and humbling for me to come face to face against how much I did not know. I often wondered what my professional colleagues would think of me if I admitted to them that I needed help in solving particular problems. It was important, albeit difficult, for me to learn to acknowledge my weaknesses without apology or shame. Honesty and openness can be the keys to genuine professional behavior. Learning to say "I don't know" can be the beginning point of refining one's skills.

2. Living with problems associated with mental retardation has substantially broadened my perspective of issues which must be addressed by professionals in interacting with families. Most formal training programs are extremely limited in preparing professionals to interact meaningfully with parents of retarded children in helping them solve very practical, day-to-day problems. In my formal training at three different universities, I cannot recall considering issues such as guardianship, helping brothers and sisters of retarded children understand the nature and implications of their siblings' handicap, helping retarded children make friends in their neighborhood and community, and ways to handle situations in public when strangers stare at and mock a retarded person.

In regard to this last issue, a stranger yelled across a restaurant at my husband and me, "What's wrong with that strange little boy?" When we tried to ignore him, he kept pressing, "I asked you why that little boy looks and acts so strange." Other persons in the restaurant looked back and forth between him and us, waiting for a response. My husband told him that nothing was wrong and for him to mind his own business. The stranger replied, "That little boy can't talk for himself. You are an insincere man, and you have a strange little boy." The stranger left the restaurant. My husband and I were in a state of shock. Jay was unaware of the nature of the interaction. As we continued to feel the other customers looking at us and at Jay, we got up and left the restaurant. How is the best way for parents to handle such situations? It was hard enough for the three of us to experience that kind of incident on a shared basis; what will happen when Jay encounters that kind of insensitivity when he is alone? How can we prepare him to handle it when we are at a loss in handling it ourselves? I did not realize the extent to which negative attitudes and society's curiosities were directed toward retarded individuals and their families until Jay came into my life.

As a teacher trainer, I have substantially reordered priorities in preparing students to work with mentally retarded persons and their families. One project which evolved from the reoriented priorities was carried out in the course, Psychology of Mental Retardation, which I taught to juniors. Rather than having students do the routine term papers or journal abstracts, I required them to develop a one-to-one citizen advocacy relationship with a retarded individual and to keep a diary of their experiences, questions, insight, and concerns. The advocacy relationship was to be like a friendship involving activities such as participating in community recreation opportunities, going shopping, riding public transportation, preparing meals together, listening to music, constructing art projects, providing respite care, or simply visiting with each other. The advocacy projects proved to be a powerful training tool (Turnbull, 1977). The students reported learning far more from experiential contacts than from traditional methods of instruction. The firsthand opportunity of getting to know a retarded person and his family as people rather than as students or clients enabled the special education trainees to become aware of some of the complexities of handicapping conditions that are rarely considered in university courses.

What goes on in training programs in the name of education is sometimes shocking. It has become very prevalent in special education departments of colleges and universities to offer courses on working with parents. I cringe at the thought of some of the course syllabi I have reviewed. In many of these courses, very limited attention is directed toward helping parents solve the day-to-day problems which almost invariably are encountered, yet weeks are devoted to the "psychological insight approach to parental guilt." Many such courses are a fraud and tend to insure further conflict and unsatisfactory relationships between parents and professionals. Extended practicum with families of handicapped children and the provision of respite care for families should be standard requirements for courses which purport to prepare students for working with parents.

3. When professionals interact with parents, respect is a necessary ingredient. For too long, the professional-parent relationship has been characterized by a superiority (professional)-inferiority (parent) interaction. Professionals often have tended to interact with parents based on what they think the parent needs rather than by responding to the needs stated by the parents. Sometimes this situation results from the professional not being willing to take the time to listen actively to what the parent is saying. Some professionals establish the posture of immediately giving advice rather than spending time getting a grasp of the problem. One of the most meaningful interactions I have had as a parent with a professional since Jay has been home was with a psychologist. As I shared some very personal concerns with her related to planning for Jay's future, tears came down her cheeks. We sat in silence for a long time, both considering the course of action which would be in Jay's best interest. The silence was beautiful. It confirmed that she was hearing what I was saying and was sharing my feelings on the subject. There was no easy answer. An immediate response, telling me not to worry about things, would have insulted my sensibilities. I knew she respected me when she poignantly shared my feelings. The result of that interaction was that my respect for her as a professional grew one hundredfold.

Many offhand comments offer insights into the professional's views of parents. One special educator asked me if I knew of handicapped children she might tutor in the summer who were achieving not more than two years below grade level. She commented that parents of children achieving at a lower level probably would not be interested in paying for tutoring, since they would likely be the type of parents who had spent their lives wishing their problems away. That type of callous generalization indicated that the teacher had limited respect for parents of handicapped children. And she was clearly passing her biases along to anyone who might listen. For a period of time I was unsure of how to handle this kind of unprofessional behavior of professionals. In some cases, I was so surprised that I found myself at a loss in responding. I have come to the conclusion that an immediate response, asking the professional to clarify and support what he means, is appropriate. In most cases I have found that the professional does not really mean what he has said. However, bringing insidious comments about parents to the attention of professionals will result in their thinking twice before making such comments in the future.

4. A parent-professional partnership is essential if handicapped children are to be provided with opportunities to reach their full potential. Parents cannot assume all the responsibilities alone. After Jay returned home, Rud and I found ourselves consumed with fulfilling advocacy responsibilities which we felt were our duty as parents of a retarded child. We had meetings on an average of four or five nights a week. We were actively involved with the Association for Retarded Citizens, group home and sheltered workshop board of directors, day-care coalition, a special education task force for the local schools, and a coalition aimed at legislative impact. We were constantly on the go and hardly had any time at all for family relaxation. It occurred to us that we had brought Jay home from the institution only to leave him with a baby sitter for an inordinate amount of time while we went out and advocated for him. I could not help but wonder why I saw so few of my professional colleagues who espoused beliefs in the importance of advocacy during work hours at these evening meetings. Rud and I began to question whether the concept of normalization applies to families of handicapped individuals as well as to handicapped persons themselves. There was nothing normal about our schedules. We were not just consumers, rather we were *consumed* by the need to establish programs and services for Jay. Once we reached the point of exhaustion and frustration, we realized that family priorities had to take precedence over advocacy needs.

Just as parents cannot meet all the needs of their handicapped child, neither can professionals. Often parents do not do their fair share in helping their child and leave overriding responsibility to the professional. Parents and professionals must work together in mutually defining and sharing roles and responsibilities, so no one becomes overwhelmed with the task to be accomplished.

5. Too often the need for handicapped children to have personal relationships with individuals outside of the family is overlooked. In the three years since Jay has been home, he has very rarely been invited by other children (handicapped and nonhandicapped) to participate in activities. Almost all of his recreational alternatives revolve around family activities or inviting neighborhood friends over to the house to play with him. Parents often need help in knowing how to increase socialization options for their handicapped child who is not automatically accepted by others (Turnbull, in press).

One of the nicest things that has happened to us since Jay's return home has been his relationship with "Grandma Dot," a friend living nearby who "adopted" Jay as her "grandson." Having no grandchildren of her own, she wanted to spend time with children and asked me if she could act as a grandmother to Jay and Amy, our two-year-old daughter. I was thrilled with the idea. Grandma Dot takes Jay and Amy on outings, makes puppets with them, reads books to them, and has them over to her house to spend the night. It is one of the most enjoyable relationships that Jay has ever had. He loves to be with Grandma Dot and talks about her every day. Especially since all of our extended family live far away, it has also been very supportive for me to have her close by. I can share my feelings very openly with her and know that she understands. Additionally, it is important for me as a parent to have other persons outside of relatives who love Jay and seek opportunities to be with him. It confirms that Jay is as lovable to others as he is to us. I should add that Grandma Dot is a professional whose career is directed at working with families of handicapped children and training other professionals for such involvement.

Moving from a professional to a parent role has been a sometimes painful and difficult task for me. It has caused me to engage in tremendous self-examination. Being Jay's mother has also resulted in an extended growth process for me. As much as anything, I have learned how much I do not know. Now, I am ready to learn.

References

Turnbull, A. P. Citizen advocacy in special education training. *Education and Training of the Mentally Retarded,* 1977, *12,* 166–169.

Turnbull, A. P. Professional-parent interactions. In M. Snell (Ed.), *Curriculum for the moderately and severely handicapped.* Columbus, Oh.: Charles E. Merrill Publishing Co., in press.

Kathryn Morton

Kathryn Morton is the director of Family and Community Services of the Montgomery County [Maryland] Association for Retarded Citizens. Her previous positions include serving as research associate for Closer Look and as assistant director and director of the Information Center for Handicapped Children [funded under a grant from the Bureau of Education for the Handicapped]. She was a member of the National Advisory Committee of the Study on the Classification of Exceptional Children.

She is the mother of five daughters. Beckie, her youngest, is fifteen years old and profoundly retarded; she attends a special school in Delaware.

Identifying the Enemy – A Parent's Complaint

Raising a child who is profoundly retarded hasn't been easy, but on the other hand, it hasn't been as hard as it might have been. In balance, life has been very good to me. But I have encountered some enemies, and they need exposing. One is fatigue, and the other is loneliness.

The first doesn't need any explanation; it just needs to be taken seriously by us parents and by the professionals who advise us. Disabled children use up enormous amounts of their parents' physical and psychic energy. Our children require more of everything, and those who take parenting seriously give it to them. Yet all the rest of life goes on and also demands its due from us. And the collective demands must be accomplished within the same twenty-four-hour day allotted to everyone.

But there is more to it than just that. There is an expectation by others that we should live "normally," as if, in fact, there were nothing unnormal about our lives. Who—besides another parent of a handicapped child—understands the extraordinary effort it takes to hang onto friends, respond to family, attend back-to-school nights, take children to dentists, entertain for husbands, shop for groceries, do the housework, take the car to be fixed, drop one child off to play with a friend, pick up another after a piano lesson, or, heaven forbid, hold down a job while attending to the needs of a child who is disabled and needs extraordinary care?

It is not a one-time demand. We all know mothers whose children are recuperating from illnesses or other temporary catastrophies. Those mothers get reprieve from life's daily expectations. Husbands will shop for groceries, a friend can drive in the car pool that week, the dentist appointment can be postponed, the piano lesson canceled, back-to-school night skipped. But there is nothing temporary about the catastrophic demands on time and energy made by a retarded child, and one cannot expect friends and family to respond endlessly to a crisis which is chronic. Each day presents us with the challenge of figuring out how to do everything that would be done if we didn't have a handicapped child, while managing the handicapped child who we clearly do have.

That might entail, for instance, grocery shopping with the retarded child in tow. When Beckie was little, such an excursion required only the extra energy needed to carry her on my hip and choose groceries one-handed, or the skill of maneuvering her special stroller with one hand and the grocery cart with the other. But when she hit the teens, a completely new ingredient entered the challenge. I took her shopping with me only if I felt up to looking groomed, cheerful, competent, and in command of any situation, so that when she bellowed and stamped with joy as she always did when we walked through the supermarket door, people who stared could quickly surmise that I would handle the situation, quiet my strange child, and get on with my shopping. To look as tired and preoccupied with surviving as I so often felt would be to turn *both* of us into objects of pity, and that I clearly did not need. If I could not play the role of the coping, competent mother, I did better to stay at home and grocery shop after she went to bed, or ask one of the other children to come home early and "sit" for me, or leave the big shopping until another day and ask a neighbor to pick up a necessity or two for me, or make do with what I had until I felt more energetic, though chances were excellent that I wouldn't.

The fact of life for parents of handicapped children which is least understood by others is this: It is difficult and exhausting to live normally, and yet we must. To decide on the other route, to admit that having a disabled child makes us disabled persons, to say no to the ordinary requirements of daily living is to meet the second enemy — loneliness. It means drifting slowly out of the mainstream of adult life. In a very real sense, we are damned if we do make the extraordinary effort required to live normally, and damned if we don't.

The sapping of energy occurs gradually. The isolation it imposes does, too. As I work professionally with young mothers, I see them coping energetically with the demands of everyday life. They are good parents, caring ones, doing everything possible to help their retarded child reach his potential, sometimes doing more than they have to; and if they have other children, they are doing the same for them. Most of them even get out, see friends, attend meetings, volunteer in the community, do all the things their friends and families expect them to do. All this is at least possible when one's child is little, though it demands enormous energy. But to look at the mothers of children who have turned into teen-agers is to see the beginnings of the ravages. Their life style is changing. They go out less, see few people, do less for their children. They are stripping their living to the essentials. And to look at parents of retarded adults still living at home is to *know* that their lives are very different from their peers. The physical and psychic effects of twenty or more years of extraordinary demands on their energies are visible, and they have given up the struggle to be "normal." The enemies are related. In the very long run, energy dwindles and a way of life sets in that is plainly isolated.

There is much about parenting a handicapped child which makes it a lonely business. First of all, there are too few retarded children to give them the advantage of being commonplace. And ignorance about them still abounds — about their diversity, about services which can help them, and about the problems their parents and siblings face. Even the best-intentioned people, trying hard to be helpful on the basis of bits and scraps of information they have gleaned from an occasional magazine article or TV program, can make parents feel very much alone and unhelped. I cannot count the number of times that I have been informed about wonderful schools, dedicated people, heretofore undiscovered cures, which can help my child. I have been enthusiastically referred over a dozen times to St. Coletta's in Wisconsin "where the Kennedy daughter is." It is always painful to deal with the disappointment of the person when I point out that St. Coletta's does not accept children who are as severely retarded as mine. It is as if I am somehow being uncooperative and do not want to be helped. But in all fairness, I should not resent and blame them for their limited knowledge. I must understand that it is only human to feel impotent and impatient with problems which have no immediate cure, no prompt solution, no easy answers.

I can still feel rage with the stranger in the public library who, years ago, commented on the four year old I was carrying, suggesting that I let her walk. I explained that she couldn't walk, that she was severely retarded. The stranger's face softened; her attitude was warm and understanding. "Oh," she said, "they are such wonderful children, and all they need is loving." Perhaps I had a premonition even then of how many years of assistance and training it would take before she would be able to walk, not to mention toilet herself, feed herself, and dress herself which she still cannot do at age fifteen. One comes out of such interviews feeling very much alone, burdened by the obligation to explain, educate, and reassure others because they know so little about our children and so very little about how to help.

There may be no solution to our dilemma. As one looks down the list of life's other sad happenings, most bring with them a ritual or a tradition which helps people deal with them. When a person is ill, there are cards to send, visits to make, flowers to deliver, gifts that comfort. When someone dies, there are routine ways of informing people of the sad news, there are funerals where people can grieve together, and there is a long period of mourning during which being sorrowful is O.K., in fact expected. Friends and acquaintances know their roles—to be sympathetic, understanding, comforting, available when needed, and helpful in managing the mechanics of living during the grieving period. It is only after many months that the surviving members of the family are expected to lay aside their grief and resume normal living. All those rituals and expectations are helpful. The roles of the comforter and the comforted are clear-cut.

The birth and life of a retarded child has no such advantages. It is a quasi-tragedy, a joyful event that got spoiled. There is no established way of announcing the case for grief felt, in fact no real certainty that one is entitled to out-and-out grieving, since it takes time before anyone can know just how severe the disability is. One should not be gloomy and expect the worst. But there is certainly little reason to feel happy. Family and friends are faced with the same ambivalence. Just what is their role? What words should they say? Can they reassure that everything will be all right? Should they extend their sympathy on this sad occasion? bring supper to the family? send flowers? None of the usual comforting gestures are appropriate, and most people, under such circumstances, do and say nothing. The absence of response to an event of such enormous significance and impact on the lives of the parents simply compounds their loneliness.

This loneliness is not a one-time phenomenon. I suspect that the behavior of the members of my family is typical. Most of my relatives do not talk about Beckie with me; from their point of view there is really not much to say after the initial "too bad"-ness has been expressed. But since the concern and care for her goes on and on in my life, leaving the topic unmentioned is to treat a major segment of my mental and emotional life as unmentionable. And that is very isolating. One hears the disappointment expressed again and again when mothers of retarded children assemble—in instance after instance of family members *not* providing the ongoing emotional support required. Yet, I think we are wrong to expect support to come from them. They may well be the people least able to provide it because their own discomfort is so acute. Each of them is having to come to terms with the why's of the arrival of a retarded child as the son or daughter of someone they love and care about. It is very likely true, however, that those who are able to find an answer which satisfies them are less uncomfortable, more able to talk about the child, more able to be helpful, than those who have not. Beckie's grandmother's distress and discomfort was acute for years until I turned professional and began writing for and working with families of handicapped children. Then she saw it all in terms of a mission—something intended to happen. It is not an answer I share, but it is her way of accepting Beckie as an important and significant happening, and I find the ease with which she can now deal with the child comforting and companionable.

The potential for loneliness is present every step of the way. The process of referral to specialists thrusts parents outside the mainstream of help. For the parent whose child is in a special education class, even such a commonplace event as a PTA meeting can be a difficult experience. Chances are good that not much that's relevant to the special class will be discussed. Chances are also good that what goes on at the PTA meetings will become less and less interesting to the parent of the child in the special class, and motivation to join in will dwindle. Bit by bit it is easy to have less and less in common with parents who do not have handicapped children. Perhaps special classes, special schools, special buses, and even our special parent organizations are ultimately doing as much to segregate and isolate parents from the mainstream of adult life as they isolate children from the mainstream of child-life.

There is really no solution for us parents except to put out the extraordinary effort it takes to live normally, to keep one leg in the mainstream, to explain, educate, reassure the others, to be up to taking our children wherever we go. It's a lot to ask of the parent whose energies are extraordinarily burdened.

If only new traditions, new rituals, could be invented to help others deal with our particular kind of sad happening! If only practical offers of help were a traditional response to handicapped children—offers to baby-sit while we grocery shop, offers to take our children for a walk around the block, offers to take them swimming, offers to give any reprieve, however short, which could give the parents, especially the mother, a chance to relax or tend to other things. Sympathy and pats on the back are nice, but we can get our solace most effectively from our fellow parents who do indeed fully understand. It's practical help, time, and manpower we need to put our "enemies" to rout, and those gifts must come from people who are less burdened than we.

Janet M. Bennett

Janet Bennett is the mother of four children. Kathryn, her youngest daughter, aged fifteen, has mongolism. Janet affirms that her children have been her teachers. She has worked in religious education and media reviewing and currently writes a newsletter for the National Catholic Education Association. The subjects of Janet's articles include teaching resources and handicapping conditions. Her other experiences include serving on various committees of the New Jersey Association for Retarded Citizens.

Company, Halt!

In the musical *How to Succeed in Business Without Really Trying*, the statistician Alexander Twimble describes his philosophy for success in the very conservative company he works for. In the song "The Company Way," he explains how he programs his face to smile automatically at all executives; how he consciously erases from his mind any ideas and suggestions that may try to emerge, while at the same time he rubber-stamps any directives coming from the top brass. He maintains an unswerving attitude of admiration and enthusiasm for anything the Company provides, from the menus in the cafeteria to the company stationery and magazine. Twimble sees his survival as irrevocably linked to the Company. Though it may take a good deal of effort, even a deliberate shift in personality, for Twimble it's the only possible way to guarantee his job security.

In my fifteen years as the mother of a retarded daughter, I've found that a major source of distress for parents, and a deterrent to progress for their children, is the very handicap-establishment which supposedly exists to help them. This handicap-establishment is very much like a giant corporation—sluggish, conservative, unimaginative, able to serve individuals only in limited ways. For a number of reasons which I'll try to catalogue here, most parents feel that they have no choice but to play things "the company way" in dealing with the problem of retardation.

This handicap-establishment has lots of departments, but the two chief ones affecting parents are the local associations for retarded children and public school systems. Both embody all kinds of attitudes, assumptions, and myths which generally go unchallenged in any serious fashion.

Supposed enemies without—a hostile public, recalcitrant legislators, limited funds, an apathetic parent constituency—loom so large that a very real enemy within—the philosophical and operational deficiencies of the organization or school system itself—is seldom considered. I believe that some basic premises underlying the whole enterprise, the entire handicap-establishment, ought to be looked at coldly and critically. Though probably few parents of retarded children have the time or inclination to explore these matters systematically, I'm certain that they have responded to them in bits and pieces as they've worked through their own experiences with their child. Conversations in grocery check-out lines and on commuter trains give ample evidence to support the statements which follow.

The Local Association

One reason the handicap-establishment is a problem is precisely that it *is* established. The "long rangeness" of the thing, the institutionalizing of a problem, results in a state of affairs not much different from most other organizational activities or business ventures which do not claim "help for" as a rationale, which have no humane or altruistic purpose.

Any bad news or unhappy event does certain similar things. Affected individuals huddle together in shared misery. Outsiders from a small or expanded periphery rally round to support. But sudden immediate emergencies—an accident, a fire, an illness, a death—seem to produce emotions and behaviors which are more efficient, truer, nobler than those which attend a continuing problem of diminishing dramatic impact.

Once the clear fire of basic feelings and instant needs has dampened down, the practical requirements and pedestrian details of managing a long-run difficulty are less stimulating, less interesting. As time goes on, as mechanisms are developed to deal with the problem on a continuing basis, the familiar everyday dynamics of assertiveness, competition, laziness, defensiveness, insecurity, and the like reappear. After the first heroic efforts surrounding a major disaster like a hurricane or an earthquake, you begin to hear about the organizational conflicts among international rescue or political agencies. Once a family crisis has quieted a bit, the infighting and jockeying for control or escape from duty become evident among relatives.

Parents of retarded children are often dismayed when they first attend an ARC unit business meeting. In the early days of trying to cope with the new awareness of retardation, parents often need—and need to believe in—a warm and caring fraternity of other parents. Yet, frequently they find that parents who serve on the unit's governing board behave with all the brittle competitiveness of business or politics.

For a year or more I served on one of these executive boards and listened with fascination, amusement, and frustration to the wrangling that characterized most meetings. A fellow board member whispered to me in disgust one evening: "These are all people who get crapped on all day at work, and this organization gives them the chance to crap on somebody else in the evening." Though an ARC unit claims to be bent on serving the needs of parents and their children, it is these parents and their children who are, directly or indirectly, the ones who are "crapped on."

The idea behind parent organizations is that in union there's strength. The many inadequacies of legislation, education, public opinion, could, it was thought, be overcome by the concerted efforts of a solid front of parents. Support gained along the way from the community and from professional people in the field of mental retardation, medicine, education, or public service (like the Kennedys or Humphreys) would add to the parents' credibility and clout. As hoped-for programs were adopted by schools and government, the parent associations conceivably would be able to phase themselves out of existence.

To accomplish major goals, minor ones are often sidetracked. Major goals must be argued about and modified, often compromised quite drastically, in order to stand a chance of acceptance. What happens ultimately is that large, long-range goals for a lot of parents compete with smaller, short-term goals for single families, for a single child. Laws, classes, federal grants all depend on the many, not the one.

Often only moderate gains are made, and only slowly, and seldom are these gains achieved in time to benefit those people who initiated them. In medieval times, men of great faith could undertake to build a cathedral, knowing that it would not be completed until after they, and probably their children, had died. For many people, the vision of progress for retarded people is rather like this noble vision of eventual success, but individual parents and individual children cannot afford to sacrifice a personal vision while the universal vision evolves.

The slow process of effecting change modifies people as well as ideas and plans. Those parents who have been active and involved for a long time, who have been instrumental in promoting change, often acquire or claim a semiprofessional status, with all the potential power hazards such status implies. As they work through the necessary buffing and polishing of the large issues on local, state, or national committees, and as they endure their own personal buffing through the experiences of their own retarded child, their original feelings, their individualized convictions, undergo gradual alteration. In too many cases, the long-time parent is indistinguishable from the professional he may once have opposed; he is in greater or lesser measure out of touch with his own instincts and the recollection of the hot-off-the-experience needs and emotions he felt as a new parent. Indeed, the satisfaction and status such parents derive through these activities are often the very palliatives which help to modify the initial impact of having produced a child who is retarded.

Length of service is one reason for the dilution of progress even as progress appears to be made. The routine joining or belonging to a local association has mixed benefits. The most common reason for joining a local unit is the initial desperate need for reassurance and information. These two needs are met in varying degrees.

In a random mix of parents at a meeting, it's likely that there will be one or two individuals with the unique kind of empathy, tact, wit, insight, and intelligence to perform for the other parents that miracle of healing that can come only through personal contact. Further, just the appearance of survivors—people who get their hair frosted, talk of movies they've seen, fret about slipcover material or stubborn carburetors—can have subliminal curative effects. Even the afore-mentioned administrative squabbling can at times be evidence for a shattered parent that he will someday have more on his mind than this one all-encompassing tragedy.

Information is another matter. When I joined an ARC unit fifteen years ago, I learned all they could tell me about mongolism in about ten minutes. The regular programs of speakers and films only end-lessly rearranged these same few basic statements. The "library" was a cluttered mess, with nothing catalogued even under major subject headings.

Most of what I learned in that period came from informal, after-the-meeting conversations with a small group of equally novice mothers. Our own persistent reading, dogged research, and speculation began to piece together a fairly solid portrait of the problem. The rest of my learning came from my own volunteer activities with the unit as newsletter editor, column writer, program and publicity chairman, chiefly because in these capacities I had the leverage to command important people who knew things to talk to me and answer my questions.

Several other members also saw information gathering as a necessary activity. As I did, they understood information to mean specific details about medical causes and treatment, educational options and approaches, continuous assessment of day-to-day or future experience and expectations. They independently provided occasional summary reports on particular significant points.

Though the rhetoric of the organization appeared to agree about the job of making information available, in practice most information the organization itself made available had to do with details about maintaining its own structure (fund raising, paying dues, etc.) or programs (dates and times of meetings, transportation schedules, deadlines for filing forms). I was astonished when, only a month after I joined the unit, the director called to ask me how to go about institutionalizing a retarded child. (In my original phone call I had said that I had investigated this process on my doctor's advice.) How in the world could a county association not know this? How could I, a newcomer to the problem, know more than those constantly in touch?

Granted, this was a while ago. Things may have improved. I no longer belong to a parent association. But I have friends who do, and I occasionally read through copies of their associations' newsletters. From my reading and from their comments, very little seems to be different from what it was then. A little information, a lot of public relations, a few reports, a lot of pictures of civic leaders presenting checks.

Some parents find, as I did, that active participation in the organization is a way of finding out what they need to know, but most parents assist the organization for other reasons. In the mythology of the handicap-establishment, "getting involved" is the mark of a good parent. The organization is, the newsletter repeatedly reminds you, *your* organization.

A related bit of mythology trades on the image of fraternity. A parent must leap from personal grief and concern to a posture of generalized concern, a passionate commitment to the interests of *all* children with handicaps everywhere. A booklet widely distributed in the sixties in fact proposed that turning outward in service to the larger community of retarded people represented the approved final stage in the development of a parent. By implication, parents who tarried on the way to this goal were made of poor stuff or were plain selfish, doubtless wallowing in their misery.

Such guilt inducing is rampant. "It's always the same few," whine newsletters and nominating committees and unit presidents at meetings. In the white heat of grief and confusion when a new parent approaches a local association, any directives or suggestions can make a lasting imprint. New parents cast about for signals—they want to know how to proceed. Social creatures that they are, they want to know how to behave as well. In this strange uncharted territory, they try to do as they're asked, do as the other veteran parents do.

My first phone call to my local unit produced a pleasant-enough response from the office secretary and a promise of some "information" to be mailed. This material duly arrived. It consisted of a short summary of the unit's programs and services and a long questionnaire on which I could indicate areas for which I would be delighted to volunteer. There were numberless areas where I would be useful to the unit; there seemed little they had to offer me. The meetings sounded dull and preoccupied with large and small bureaucratic issues; nothing seemed to have a bearing on Kathryn's development until a nursery class which she could attend three years hence. The message was clear: A parent in my circumstances, trying to cope with a trauma of uncertain dimensions, should marshal her forces, muster her energies, and get out and work for the cause.

This message of duty lingers on in the consciousness. I've watched numberless parents driven by its nagging whisper to constant activity year after year—committees, collections, raffles, dances, bowling parties, etc. Others can't or won't follow this route, but the accusing murmur goes on, a scolding conscience implanted like a pacemaker. The language and methods, urging cooperation, responsibility, and loyalty, are exactly the same as those of the PTA, the YMCA, the Girl Scouts, and churches. But somehow the burden of guilt is heavier because of the prevailing atmosphere of inter-relationship, interdependency. A retarded child initiates us into a cosmic fraternity—we're all one, we're all linked together like blood brothers, we're all responsible for everything that happens. God, what a burden! Isn't one burden, dumped on us by fate, quite enough? Must we have the added load of organizational busy-work, presented as though each of us is a finger in the dike without which all the sad-eyed retarded children in the world will drown?

A retarded child is generally an immediate and continuing drain on body, mind, pocketbook, and time. Too many parents find their already overextended resources further taxed by this sense of obligation to the organization. Some, of course, are affected quite differently; for them the organization provides escape from the realities of a retarded child while giving a consoling sense of "doing something." For others, the committee work and officerships give a new identity and status which would never have been their lot otherwise. For still others, work for an ARC unit is only a more logical choice from the variety of such activities in which they normally engage anyway out of natural civic enthusiasm.

Regardless of motivation, or whether helping the unit is a pleasure or a trial, should most parents be doing this work at all? Most parents today have more than they can handle under ordinary circumstances. Schools, with their lunches, forms, permission slips, conferences, back-to-school nights, homework, projects, concerts, and athletics, run an ordinary household ragged through most of the year. Viruses, broken bones, and rashes complicate things in between. And bills and in-laws and job demands keep up a constant current of worry. How can *any* group dare to make *any* parent feel guilty about lack of social responsibility, let alone parents with a significant extra problem such as retardation?

At the time of Kathryn's birth I also had to manage the school schedules of Amanda who was in the sixth grade and Peter, in the second grade, which were timed to overlap with and consequently conflict with Martha's kindergarten hours. Between 11:30 and 12:30 each day I had to feed one child, pick up two, drop off one, feed three, drop off two. Kathryn's naps had to fit in wherever they could; the timing of breast-feeding was an interesting challenge. I was recovering from a combined Caesarean delivery and hysterectomy, and while trying to manage my own lunches along with the others, unwittingly encouraged attacks from a developing hernia.

If I had had an *un*retarded baby, I'd never in a million years have thought of volunteering for anything during that period. Now that I had Kathryn, why in the world would I be expected to do anything of the kind? Yet in the face of minimal help from the organization, it was telling me I should help it. And, numb with shock and diminished self-confidence, I did my best to comply.

All kinds of groups—churches not the least among them—display this inversion of roles. Instead of being served by the organization, members are required to serve, but it isn't just the unfairness of this that I object to. It's an even more subtly damaging problem.

In the process of belonging to and working for an association dedicated to retardation, parents join hands with fate. They cement their own identity as parents of retarded children; they wed themselves to the problem through a myriad of meetings and mailings; they immerse themselves in a society of people like themselves. As I mentioned earlier, there are differences in the immediate and long-range effects of any behavior. While it is probably inevitable, and often helpful, for parents to be caught up in a parents' group in the beginning, such close and constant attachment and identification fairly soon reaches a point of diminishing returns. After that, I believe the process can have a damaging impact on the parents and on the child's future.

Early on I decided that I would *not* be a parent of a retarded child. I would resist the tendency to alter my fundamental identity in recognition of the twist in the road that had come with retardation. The road might have twisted, but it was still the same I who walked the road. Kathryn was *not* "a mongoloid" nor was she later on that equally invasive "child with Down's syndrome." She was a child, she was Kathryn, and she *had* mongolism, or whatever name; I didn't care what anyone cared to use to describe her condition. An ARC unit or any other kind of group could offer me services or information or moral support or advice, but it would not provide me—or Kathryn— with an identity.

I believe that the very personal disappointment and discouragement, and close-to-home practical difficulties of handling a retarded child are quite enough to manage. I think, in most cases, the change in parents' perception of themselves, of who they are, is both destructive and permanent. Close and continuing relationship to an association devoted to retardation can only give constant reinforcement to this perception, can only guarantee that there will be no return to the "Who I was before." Indeed, in the establishment mythology, "acceptance" is a major goal, and acceptance means taking the fact of retardation into your consciousness and making it part of you.

I recently watched a young woman in a shoe store as her mongoloid daughter marched up and down among the racks, humming, clapping her hands, talking to her image in the mirror. Every bone, muscle, and nerve in the mother's body was concentrated on the task of appearing composed, at ease, unembarrassed. Somehow it seemed that just being the child's mother was not enough, not the major task. What was more important was the role of "well-adjusted parent," of conveying the message to an ever-observing public that she was managing, she was doing well; it was not getting her down. Yet the tension in her pose, the studied casualness with which she noted the youngster's activity—constantly keeping an eye on the possibility of shoe boxes becoming overturned, while she earnestly engaged the clerk in discussion of various styles—presented a picture of someone very hard at work in service to a relentless awareness.

Exactly like the nervous mother in church who gradually makes everyone else uneasy about the quite normal and inoffensive wiggling of a small child, this mother's awareness and concentration were almost palpable and certainly contagious. I found myself watching rather nervously to see what might happen, and so did Kathryn who was sitting beside me. But this mother and her mongoloid daughter who was almost the same age as Kathryn were not conscious of us—not, I think, because Kathryn was sitting quietly and the other girl was moving about. I'm certain it was because the mother's self-consciousness kept her totally absorbed while at the same time it was being transmitted through the room on extrasensory waves.

I took out my notebook and scribbled a reminder to myself: *Don't ever cast yourself in the role of well-adjusted parent. It's too much work.* It was an interesting reminder, because I had once attempted the same process as this woman in the shoe store.

Under handicap-establishment tutelage, a major portion of parents' psychic energy goes to learning the clues to good adjustment, total acceptance. Parents learn to avoid at all cost behavior that will earn a charge of "not facing reality." What this means is constant, unremitting inner awareness of the fact that retardation exists in their household. They've been initiated into a lodge, with life-long membership, and any thought of keeping their distance would be traitorous.

Instead of saying "initiated," it might be more correct to say "hooked." Consider the image of beleaguered but dedicated parents toiling selflessly for a cause, their efforts the more effective because of the poignancy of personal pain. This image is an appealing one for parents who need to see some redemptive value in the disheartening experience of having a retarded child. In the religious traditions we consult in times of tragedy, self-sacrifice has always been represented as noble; but the image of zealous parents is also a useful one for organizations, for willing volunteer parents are the necessary organizational fodder to keep the whole thing going once it's started. (The children themselves, whether it's admitted or not, are in the same category.)

The original concept of parent organization is, of course, barely true today. Though ARC units began as parent groups, now only a few parents are in any way the moving spirit behind them. Instead they defer to the association's executive director (probably a paid professional with generalized social service or fund-raising credentials), the board (usually now consisting of prominent community leaders as well as parents), the programs of the state and national organizations, and the requirements of state and federal legislation. The general membership of parents is instructed in matters concerning them; told what they are expected to do; scolded about contributing, paying dues, volunteering, "getting involved." They are also commanded to be grateful for all the organization's programs, and to recognize their superior quality, which is undeniable by virtue of the fact that these programs are presented under the organization's sponsorship.

In my own experience with the preschool class in which I dutifully enrolled Kathryn at age 3½, the quality was decidedly *not* good. But the fact that it was there at all, that it met state requirements for cleanliness and safety, was furnished with fashionable and approved equipment, and was staffed with dedicated personnel was evidence of quality to the consumer. Nonetheless, regardless of conformity to guidelines, I found the philosophy oppressive and full of clichés, and the routines restrictive, yet it took me eight months to acknowledge the validity of my own instincts sufficiently to take Kathryn out, and several years to overcome my sense of guilt at not having been properly grateful for the fact that the class was offered and that Kathryn had been admitted. After all, aren't parents supposed to take advantage of everything that's offered for retarded children? Wasn't there a waiting list of parents eager and ready to do just that? Who did I think I was, being fussy in a situation like this?

Like labor unions, local associations began in an effort to remedy abuses and to provide needed benefits, but, like unions, they have become dogmatic institutions themselves. In the commitment to the good of a large anonymous constituency, the welfare of individuals is diminished. In recruiting parents into the service of the organization, the parents' energies are siphoned away from their primary concern—their own child, their own family. The undercurrent reminding parents to be grateful keeps parent criticism at a low pitch. And, most important, the identity nourished by the association limits the parents' ability to analyze and judge anything except in relation to retardation.

Public School Classes

The other major deparment of The Company, public school classes, has characteristics equivalent to those of the parent association. This department is even more complex because of the many influences it harbors within itself and because it provides its own mutations for the influences which originate in the local association. Such complexity means that I can only skim the surface here.

Parent gratitude has always been a part of the public school's picture of the "good parent"; this image has been used since the beginning of time to ensure good order. "Good parents" are the ones who do certain things like providing enriching experiences at the library and museum, assuring stimulating dinner conversation, and understanding question-answering sessions for their offspring, all aimed at developing a well-mannered, eager, cooperative, and industrious pupil ready for the school's ministrations. "Bad parents" simultaneously ignore and indulge their children, as they devote themselves to career building or carousing at country clubs. They likewise ignore the school's requirements until such time as the child, predictably, fails his lessons or turns bad. Then, naturally, they blame the school for its shortcomings and shout dramatically: "But he's a good boy—I gave him everything!"

All parents must be grateful for the long hours and dedication of teachers and administrators whose declared vocation is to work closely with the home in tugging the eager/reluctant, scholar/under-achiever, model child/delinquent on into the college of his choice or, against the ego requirements of the pushy mother or father bent on producing a surgeon, into a good honest job where he can find his true calling in working with his hands. Parents of retarded children must in addition be thankful for the even more heroic dedication of inspired or fantastic teachers, special classes, a mixed bag of specialists (psychologists, social workers, audiologists, speech therapists, etc.) and, where it's happening, mainstreaming. What it boils down to is that they're supposed to be, and generally are, grateful that their retarded children are included, allowed in on what "regular" kids take for granted, even if the process requires that they submit to being "treated to death," as Ivan Illich, a theorist on reform, suggests, by a whole industry of "biocrats."

From the diagnosis on of a child's retardation, the handicap-establishment trains parents of retarded children to be so occupied with their problem, always conscious of the specialness of their kids and themselves, that they either haven't time or don't dare to figure out what they really want and whether that's what they're getting. From beginning to end their vision is riveted on and limited to the retardedness of things. The doubtless quite suitable defensiveness that characterized the beginnings of parent organizations when it was true that enough was not done for these children, continues uninterrupted even when all kinds of things *are* being done. But are they the right things?

Whether parents like or dislike their children's special classes, they're held back from voicing criticism by oblique reminders of the early days when there were no classes at all. (Those were the days, remember, when closets and attics across the land presumably harbored a supply of sluggish and slovenly retarded children.) After a long Christmas holiday when the youngster goes back to his class, parents say with relief, "Well, it's better than nothing." Just the term "special class" somehow suggests concession and a veiled threat that if parents get picky, the class will just be eliminated. It's obviously illegal, obviously not going to happen; but the nagging primordial fear stays alive among parents just the same.

The advantages of special segregated classes for children of supposedly similar intellectual ability or with physical or psychic idiosyncrasies which permit category grouping have been increasingly challenged by thoughtful individuals in education and other fields. Nonetheless, the wholesale trucking of children to centralized special classes continues. Every day I pass little vans with their odd little cargo as they crisscross the countryside, taking this one from here to there and that one from there to here. An hour-long bus trip is not unusual even for children who, by definition, have reduced physical endurance.

The quality of classes, once the children get where they're going, is variable. In any number of recommended reconnaissance tours I've made, such classes have not been impressive. They are either perpetual nursery schools for oversize tots or regular schools chopped up in little pieces and run through a projector at slow speed. "Innovative techniques" promoted by the education industry's obsession with "methodology" look good to the constituents and the school board, and keep the young teachers amused, but little of real value seems to occur.

In one class I visited, about eight young children designated trainable were lined up on chairs to watch that favorite of today's educators, a filmstrip. It was a Disney instructional piece, intended to present the facts about food production and distribution. It careened from a farm and tractors to some kind of warehouse or cannery, then on to a grocery store with shopping carts. The message might have concerned mechanization or transportation, although the narrator, in classic filmstrip drone, occasionally mentioned something about food. All these pictures were rather small-scale realistic drawings. They were followed abruptly by illustrations of food groupings, done in more abstract style, on a scale which showed a streak covering approximately the same portion of screen as a barn and silo had required only moments before. The teacher proceeded to point out various food items, which was a good idea, since what looked like a modernistic armchair turned out to be a roast beef. She lost her bearings a few frames later as she sweetly pointed to some bumpy-looking tan things. "Look at the mushrooms," she purred, having vainly tried to identify what, since they were in a collection representing grains, were more likely meant to be Parker House rolls. It was a silly filmstrip, badly organized, attempting too much, and in no way suited to a band of youngsters who weren't too dumb to be bored to death with it. When the teacher was not trying to figure out what the filmstrip was about in order to seem in control of things, she was snapping orders to the children to sit up straight, turn around, watch the screen.

Such useless "teaching" goes on everywhere, not just in special classes, and this is the problem. Things are not well with schools in general today, as a host of education critics keeps pointing out. There's too much work, with too little significance. Too much time is spent shuffling dittoes and filling in workbook pages. These workbooks are a jumbled mess, with incomprehensible instructions and largely useless tasks. Reading lessons concentrate on decoding written material, without acknowledging that a major purpose and incentive for reading is the pleasure of enjoying good writing. Stories offered for the child to practice his reading skills are tasteless, bland, with awkward sentence construction. Trickiness masquerades as imagination; the contemporary substitutes for the valuable. Beauty is nonexistent. As critic John Leonard once said about Disney movies, "Cute is beauty, beauty cute."

I agree with John Holt's judgment that children are lucky if they get fifteen minutes of real teaching in school. From my own observations during twenty years of enduring schools with my children, it's hard not to agree with Holt's advice to keep children out of school altogether, to "let all those escape it who can, any way they can."

A nineteenth century commentator, Sydney Smith, wrote: "Some men through indolence, others through ignorance, and most through necessity, submit to the established education of the times; and seek for their children that species of distinction which happens, at the period in which they live, to be stamped with the approbation of mankind." Exactly my point for parents who have retarded children and those who don't. The former compound the felony—they are so busy insisting that they want in on regular education that they fail to notice that it's hardly worth getting in on. Who would want their children in the hands of people who make claims like this, which arrived in today's mail: "Student/teacher interactions in nonstructured, informal situations can be optimized to nurture the development of thorough and efficient thinking skills for children"?

Mainstreaming simply means that *all* kids have an equal shot at mediocre schooling. (Of course, even this is subject to discount since, like so many other educational innovations, what's claimed by public relations announcements is not always fact.) Bringing retarded children into a regular classroom does not necessarily end segregation and discrimination—it may only camouflage it.

A major problem of public education, of course, is that, while it's universally available, it's also compulsory and monopolistic. A child has to go, and he usually has to stay where he is put. Retarded children don't exactly *have* to go to school in the same sense that other children are legally bound to do so, but they are equally locked into the system once they enter it.

Children of ordinary ability, without limiting handicaps, generally have greater adapting and defending powers in the face of poor teaching. They also have greater opportunity to compensate through their homes or extracurricular activities. Retarded children's choices are even more limited, sometimes by their very inability to identify or report on an unsatisfactory classroom situation. For all children, beyond certain minor variations, a change of class means money. It means private school or tutoring. It also means time, energy, conviction.

I took the private school and tutoring route for Kathryn. Regrettably, I didn't have the insight or funds to do it for my other children, though the decline of the schools which was obvious during Amanda's first few grades accelerated rapidly during the period of Peter and Martha's attendance. In any case, since that first troublesome preschool experience, I have worked out Kathryn's schooling year by year through a variety of situations, all in the regular classes of regular schools. She has had no special class placement since the age of 3½.

First she attended a private nursery school and a private kindergarten. Then came a four-year hitch in a remarkable open-classroom situation (ninety children, four teachers) in a public school. Mostly I paid tuition, but midway in the public school years some administrative shifts meant that what had begun as a free-spirited experiment began to change into a "program." This program in which Kathryn became a pilot child for a federal grant proposal had mixed benefits. It began the inevitable deterioration of the original vision, but it also permitted my school district to assume tuition payments. Fortunately, even deterioration is subject to bureaucratic influences; the decline proceeded slowly enough to allow Kathryn to enjoy some of the original benefits for a while longer.

This year Kathryn is in a class of eight girls in a small ungraded Catholic school. In addition, as insurance against the possibility of having no suitable class available at any point, Kathryn is tutored on a rather random schedule by one of the teachers from the original public school open classroom, who retired after the demise of that fine experiment. They work on short research papers, on some of Kathryn's regular class assignments, and on expanding her writing ability. They also do needlepoint, recipes, and are about to begin rug hooking. Should we find ourselves temporarily without the kind of school we want, we would expand the tutoring as it seemed necessary.

In each instance my major purpose was to provide the interaction with nonhandicapped children which does more than any particular instructor can do to "teach" language and normal behavior patterns. In particular, such contact permits the identity "child" to take precedence over the identity "handicapped," no matter how loudly the handicapping conditions may clamor for attention.

With money you can do things—even though in our case, the money is only barely available, since it's needed at the same time as the older children's college tuitions. But what do you do if there's no money? It would certainly be a start to make low-interest loans available for *any* educational purpose, not just college expenses. The federally backed higher education loans are not ideal economic arrangements, but they would permit some options for parents who want alternatives.

All bureaucracies demand, "What do you propose?" and if you have no well-thought-out reply, your complaints are dismissed, discredited. I don't agree that the one who identifies a problem must also be the one to provide the solution. I can guess that I have appendicitis, but I doubt that it would be prudent for me to try to operate. In this instance, I do have a few observations which might be helpful.

The preceding pages have spent considerable time in outlining the problems. My recommendations are not nearly so detailed, for they proceed from a fundamental solution, a basic change in outlook, rather than from specific blueprints. This fundamental change—the shedding of the deliberate identification with retardation—permits any needed kind of change to be developed.

What would happen if parents just stopped dwelling on the fact that their children *are* retarded? Suppose they simply figured out what the children need, or are ready for, at any given time and convinced the schools—or whoever else had enough money—to provide it? I once wrote an article suggesting public libraries as alternative sources of schooling for retarded children. I still think it's a good idea.

A long time ago I stopped looking at newspaper listings of special programs for retarded children. Now I just notice what Kathryn might like. All kinds of courses are given by community schools, YMCAs, or churches. (I'm not speaking of church programs and religion classes for retarded children; these depend on the same attitudes as the schools.) Since, unlike compulsory schooling, people *choose* these classes, they are open to anyone who's interested. This holds true whether or not a fee is charged. Grandparents and teen-agers, beginners, or those with some familiarity with the subject all take the same course. Though there may be beginning, intermediate, or advanced levels, nobody would notice or care if someone took the same level course several times. For most of us and especially for retarded children, taking enough time is more important than special techniques.

Just because there is no headline or sign authorizing the admission of someone who's retarded doesn't mean that retarded people cannot consider these courses. Through the years Kathryn has been enrolled in a variety of such classes, whenever our budget and schedule would permit. She has been the only handicapped child in modern dance, twirling, and tumbling classes, where the ages ranged from four year olds to teen-agers. Currently she is in an exercise class of eight people who are high school students and housewives. The teachers, who are of all ages and backgrounds *except* special education, have been uniformly interested, unconcerned about problems Kathryn's condition might imply (none have occurred), and casual about skipping over the occasional area where she is not altogether capable. In several instances she was *not* the least able in the group.

In these classes, the subject is central. The idea is "We're teaching this. Would you like to learn it?" Obviously "*Can* you learn it?" is a factor, but this is always a factor with everyone. I would not register for violin lessons, computer programming, Russian, statistics, or ballet. A battery of tests might tell me I'm smart enough for all those things, but I am not in the least interested in them. Even though they're popular offerings, I know that for all practical purposes I would *not* be able to learn them. The mental and physical effort would be prohibitive.

Couldn't regular schools present their courses on the same basis? "Here is what we have. Who needs it?" need be the only premise. A corollary to this would be "How can we help you?"

Such a view of education obviously calls for many adjustments of facilities as well as of attitudes. The all-or-none view of scheduling and programming in which "flexibility" is as strictly defined as are rigid routines would have to go. A retarded youngster who is ready for letters and numbers, though he isn't toilet trained and can't walk, might attend one or more separate sessions in what he needs. A child with the opposite problem, mobility without academic readiness, could have physical exercises and games in the gym. If a child requires rest periods during the day, could there not be a better solution than home instruction or more space available than a cot in the nurse's office? Couldn't a day-training center be included in the space allocations, so that physical equipment could be shared by skilled athletes and those who need it for development?

Where would the staff come from? All over the place. There are plenty of former teachers, now home with babies, who would like part-time work. There's a large group of modern parents who believe in sharing the domestic duties. They, too, would work in well with the free-wheeling kind of scheduling I describe.

Curiously, we like to think that our concentration on the person is the humane way, yet it's exactly this relentless awareness of who, which translates so readily into what kind of, that dehumanizes. Paradoxically, if we look instead at what is needed, we might find that our humaneness automatically becomes more real.

No, it wouldn't be easy. We've gotten used to the shortcut of categories—"An N.I. child" (neurologically impaired) or "The C.P.s" (cerebral palsied). We've also become addicted to programs. It's no surprise to me that the words program and project begin with PR, the abbreviation for public relations. These programs for the retarded, for the elderly, for the gifted lure us farther and farther from everyone's humanity. I suggest we begin resisting the obsession with such packaging.

In the end, both parent associations and schools have one thing to offer. Associations are where parents are. Schools are where children are. Parents need other parents, and children need other children.

Except for this, everything is negotiable. Let's stop thinking that whatever happens, whatever will be accomplished, must be stamped "For the retarded." Let's stop selling our souls and our children to the company store. Let's stop playing the company way.

References

Holt, J. In R. Flaste, Embittered reformer advises: Avoid school. New York Times, April 16, 1976.

Smith, S. In J. Epstein, Bring back elitist universities. New York Times Magazine, February 6, 1977, pp. 86–8.

Dorothy Weld Avis

Dorothy Weld Avis is a psychiatric social worker at an institution for retarded individuals. She serves as a senior social work representative on a multidisciplinary professional team responsible for planning, administering, and monitoring appropriate services for three hundred severely and profoundly retarded adult clients and residents of a hospital extension unit. Her other duties include handling all nonmedical correspondence concerning residents and their families and conducting group and individual counseling sessions with clients in preparation for community placements.

Her son, Hunter, is nineteen years old and has been diagnosed as mentally retarded, autistic, and aphasic. He lives at Berkshire Village in South Egremont, Massachusetts, where he is successfully engaged in farm work and weaving.

Deinstitutionalization Jet Lag

"She'll never live to be more than a year old."
"Put him away and forget him."
"They're happier with their own kind."
"Think of the other children."
"Only professionals can give this child the kind of care and training he needs."

Families of mentally retarded or otherwise handicapped children are familiar with these phrases from the not-too-distant past. Institutional placements were made based upon these phrases and the philosophies which were behind them. The necessity for lifetime care was a basic assumption. Lives were built upon and around these ideas.

Many parents whose handicapped child was institutionalized based upon acceptance of these phrases and their assumptions are being asked to accept complete changes in expectations and assumptions. New phrases, concepts, and services are replacing the old. New programs are being implemented. Normalization, least restrictive environment, civil rights, residents' rights, parent training, and respite care are but a few.

I favor the new alternatives and philosophies. As a social worker in a large older institution, I am reminded daily of the impact these changes are having on clients, parents, and staff. I view all of the intent of new programs and the results very positively.

Discussing the impact and results of the new programs is a whole subject in itself. The impact I am choosing to discuss is the reaction of the many people who are having to change attitudes, rationales, long-held notions, and daily activities which changes in policy and philosophy have brought about. I see a similarity between the experiences these people are having and "jet lag." I call this experience in our field "deinstitutionalization jet lag."

A traveler who has zoomed at supersonic speed through several time zones finds himself physically unready for the time zone in which he lands. He is uncomfortable until his body adjusts to the portion of the day in which he is expected to fit. It takes some time and adjustment.

Experienced travelers allow for this. Clients, their families, and many staff members in institutions are having some discomfort as they adjust to the new time zone changing attitudes toward the mentally retarded require.

Inadequate communication is part of the cause of the discomfort. Families who made the decision for institutional placement long ago have a particular backlog of lack of communication which the practices of institutions through the years engendered. Thus, they have not had the opportunity to incorporate new ideas and to absorb the implications and possibilities. It is these families upon whom I would like to focus attention. I hope to remind professional people of the distance and speed we are asking families of adult, long-institutionalized clients to travel. By looking at the contrasts with which we are dealing, I hope to encourage patience and extra attempts to communicate. Our clients, and we, need the support of these families.

An elderly couple vividly illustrates the contrast between where their journey began and where they have now found themselves. Their reaction to sudden communication of new expectations includes a number of elements our original phrases and old philosophies embody. This couple came to see me during a regular visit to see their daughter in the institution. Their daughter is a woman of nearly forty who has Down's Syndrome. They had seen a television show on which an enthusiastic proponent of the community movement was a guest. They perceived his message as a promise. The message was that all clients from a given area who resided in the institution would be returned to the homes of their families or to their home area, preferably "down the street," within a year. This plan was given greater color by dramatic stories of institutional abuse.

These parents were considerably upset. They had placed their daughter in the institution as a newborn infant. This decision had been made upon the recommendation of a much respected physician. The prognosis was that the baby would live less than a year and would not develop beyond the most infantile stage. They were also told that family and friends should be told that the baby would not be coming home from the hospital and the conclusion would be that the baby had died.

Through forty years they had visited faithfully, had assumed financial responsibility, and had an affectionate relationship with their daughter. They felt they had made the only choice for her and had acted in good faith by the standards of the time.

They tearfully asked if some consideration could be given to their daughter's remaining in the institution, as it had always been her home. They feared that there would not be adequate protection and care for her in any place but the institution. They apologized for being too elderly and ill to assume her direct care. They also found it difficult to imagine how they could cope with explaining their daughter's existence after all of these years if she were placed "down the street."

There are obviously many things we could discuss about this reaction, including the couple's mechanisms for coping and more. They were expressing their reaction to their situation in an individual way. Their reaction was also colored by the only information they had up until that time about what appeared to be a new plan affecting their child and undermining their history of choices. Threatening, to be sure.

It was as if they imagined buses pulling up "down the street," depositing bewildered retarded people who were going to be living with their own or other families. Based upon the information they had, this was not too far-fetched, although literal.

The perspective of those of us closer to the situation would tell us that the range of mentally retarded clients within the institution could not be provided for so simply as a quick description of community residences would indicate. These parents didn't have that perspective.

They were considerably less anxious as they heard the explanation of how community placement comes about, how parental participation in the planning is an important ingredient, and how placements are considered on a highly individual basis. The threat turned into an opportunity for this and later discussions which were long overdue for this family that essentially had no one with whom to talk about their daughter but each other.

The new ideas had forced them to reexamine the beginning of their journey with the birth of their child, and all the years they had felt that they had done the best things for her. The sudden dramatic description of the community movement had compelled them to go through several time zones. "The baby will not live" is quite a distance from "coming home to live" forty years later.

Another family had quite a different reaction. This family had kept a very physically handicapped son at home for fifteen years. He had required nearly constant nursing care and had many serious illnesses and much out-patient therapy while at home. They, in contrast to the first family, hoped the promise would come true soon, so they could see their son more often. They raised many legitimate questions about the details of care that they knew their son needed. They wanted to know how this could be provided in the programs as they were described. The "promise" had said "all" institutional residents would be provided for. They were ready and interested in details. Their journey had started at a different point and their expectations, and their son's needs, are entirely different from the first family's needs.

Both reactions illustrate how important it is to estimate who is listening. We professional people need to listen to ourselves and the shorthand in which we sometimes speak. The communication and selling of such an important idea as one which affects so many lives deserves the careful market research which is accorded many much less important ideas. I doubt that many marketing managers would risk threatening their customers. Granted, we won't succeed if we are too timid. But let's channel our enthusiasm and urgency so that we get the most mileage for our clients . . . after we are pretty sure of where we are going.

The contrasts which can help us reflect on what we are experiencing in terms of change can be illustrated by looking at "then" and "now" in terms of institutional practices and policies. It is as if the rules of the game have changed completely. Barriers are crumbling, and a whole new set of relationships is building.

The start of this journey is the admission procedure. In the past this process began with legal papers and often court proceedings. Such things are quite intimidating to many people—regardless of their sophistication. Adding this to the emotionally charged feelings people have about their defective child, as they were called, made for a traumatic event many times.

Old admission papers which the parent was asked to sign asked for a description of "traits of character or tendencies present." The applicant was asked to underline the appropriate words. They were as follows: "Obedient, unruly, indolent, industrious, considerate, sensitive, affectionate, cruel, unstable, sexually promiscuous, sexually perverted, inadequate, thievish, untruthful." It is, at best, difficult to make a checklist to describe behavior. The vocabulary reflected the terminology of the day but was faithfully marked for infants and older people as well. Fortunately today the process is considerably more humane.

Several parents have told me that they thought that they had surrendered their child to the state when the child was admitted. They had the impression that they were no longer legally responsible for the child and had given up choices and decision making for the child. This impression would affect the quality and nature of their continuing relationship, thus creating another barrier.

There were reinforcements for the notion that the parent should keep at a distance. The institution admitted clients from a wide geographical area. Thus, transportation for visits presented problems in the days before thruways and private cars. Institutions generally have been placed outside of town and surrounded by fences. Most of us can recall driving by such places and wondering what went on inside. Surely such a place must contain something fearful as it looked so mysterious and was so far back from the road. A parent shared this kind of impression with me. Her feelings were compounded the day she actually had to drive up that drive and separate from her child at "that place." Her feelings had changed over time, but she said that there is a flashback as she approaches the drive each time she visits.

Practices within institutions seemed to separate parents from their children. Visiting hours were limited, and sometimes visits were supervised. Permissions were required. It is not too hard to interpret that this means that the child needs protection from the parents — or the reverse.

If, in the past, parents requested a home visit for their child, a social worker made a home study. Another test of standards and measuring up that parents had to weather through. Old records indicate the refusals of requests for visits in some circumstances due to housekeeping standards and other value judgments. Often the reasons given for refusals were that the child needed further training and time for adjustment. I am still not entirely sure what that meant and in some instances we might wonder what training. However, if one had accepted the rationale that only professional people could care for the child then there must be something beyond a mere parent's understanding that was going on that shouldn't be interrupted.

As if these elements aren't formidable enough, there was also the process of getting a question answered by mail. Responses to letters in some institutions always were signed by the director or superintendent. This person was usually a physician and obviously a very important person as he was responsible for such a lot of people. Some people hesitated to ask or apologized for taking his time when what they wanted was news of a child's progress.

Responses were often terse and impersonal, lacking in warmth. Letters spontaneously sent from an institution to families indicated serious illness or an accident—or a Christmas appeal, hardly welcoming, although understandable within the context of the time and the size of institutions.

Many parents persisted and remained in contact. This took some skills and tenacity. Others dropped out due to lack of ability to penetrate the barriers. Some of the latter families have been labelled as "disinterested" when overwhelmed might be a more apt description.

In our present time zone, we are still pressed by size but are trying to reestablish contact with families of clients. We are asking them, whether they be tenacious or dropouts, to join us in the present and quickly understand where we are now.

A bit of deinstitutionalization jet lag came with letters parents received several years ago when old forms of admission were changed to reflect new types of admission status. A most carefully worded letter explaining the patients' status, voluntary or otherwise, and his accompanying rights to ask to leave an institution couldn't cover the gap, of course. Many parents expressed wonderment and confusion that their now-adult child, duly labelled as in need of lifetime protection and lacking in judgment, was now granted the status to make such important decisions. The person who was now an adult was viewed as capable of making choices when the family had been assured that theirs was an eternal child.

Civil rights, voting rights, marriage, choice of where to live for someone who had been surrendered to a vegetable existence twenty years before? Correct, and correctly so. It is difficult to grasp this unassisted. Parents who were not permitted to visit on the ward are now invited to visit on the living unit, talk with staff, tour the institution, and serve as volunteers. For some, this still comes as a surprise as they had not asked to visit the ward in so many years, and we in our haste and rapid daily incorporation of the new trends may have forgotten to invite them.

The same parents who may have been considered by some to be a bit of a pest with all their questions are now serving on governing boards or overseeing committees as advocates for clients. Their suggestions are not only encouraged but are required. This *is* another time zone.

Parents are regularly invited to participate in treatment team meetings for their relative. They actively work along with the professional and direct care staff in planning for their child's program, needs, and future. Can these be the same people who were told that only professional knowledge and skill would help their child?

The staff, too, has some of the same problems of jet lag, deinstitutionalization style. Long-time employees remember when talking to a resident was to be confined to instructions. They also recall clients who worked side by side with them or for them for a few cents a week. These were the clients who became idle after a court decision on institutional peonage prevented them from working "on campus." A drastic change took place for staff and client, it was long overdue and required a shift of practices and daily roles, to be sure. The most difficult shift, I feel, is for families and employees to grasp the different practices and stance that a growth or goal-oriented view of mentally retarded people requires as opposed to the custodial model that was the norm for so long. This calls for retraining and attitudinal change. Both help in the adjustment to this time zone.

My message is that we who are in intermediary positions between the client's family and the institution should be continually mindful of where this journey began and on what premises it was accepted. We should be readily available and communicative as we are all asked to adjust to where the policies have landed us and the direction in which we are going.

We are apt to get institutionalized in our responses and bury ourselves in the inevitable paperwork that accountability and emphasis on planning places upon us. Let's not forget that there are people in those plans and they don't have an identical viewpoint or opportunity to absorb the directions and philosophies implied.

Everyone of us has a different capacity for adapting to change and for growth. Allow for this and the fact that ideas may take a different form when they are implemented into programs. Let's keep an eye on what we think we are doing and what actions we take. Do they add up to achieving the same goal?

Let's not be surprised if some families who learned to cope with the barriers we presented in the past take a while to gain confidence in the new systems and attitudes. They may take a very practical and skeptical attitude toward programs in which we see such future. They may see the today and fear that their relative, who assumes the risk, will be caught in the middle. We have an obligation to deserve their confidence.

Most of the families of older residents accepted permanent institutionalization as the only alternative, based upon the best advice available. Let us help them to accept deinstitutionalization and new concepts on the very best information available at this time, thoroughly and well communicated.

How will what we are doing now be viewed in five or ten years? There will be other time zones we, too, will have to accept. Most travelers adapt in time . . . but must everyone make the trip?

Frank Warren

Frank Warren's son, George, is fifteen years old and autistic. Frank has been a consultant to the Office for Children, North Carolina Department of Human Resources, and now is a staff member specializing in lay advocacy by parents of handi- capped [particularly autistic] persons at the Washington- based Federal Programs Information and Assistance Project. He helped establish the North Carolina Society for Autistic Children and a consumer political-action coalition, Parents and Professionals for Handicapped Children.

A Society That Is Going to Kill Your Children

To Mary Lou

Between 95 and 98 percent
of all autistic adults
are institutionalized.
(NSAC Information and
Referral Service, 1977)

Each day that you fail to advocate,
each day that you ignore an act
of discrimination, each day that you
accept another injustice, you accept
a society that is going to kill
your children. (Dussault, 1977)

It is the custom of the people in the United States to kill autistic children.

Yes. Kill them.

And it is the custom to ostracize their parents: to treat them as outcasts, as irrational men and women who do not know their own minds, who cannot tell right from wrong. Both parents and children are stripped of their rights as citizens, as if they were convicted felons who have proven that they are harmful and obnoxious to society.

How do the people kill autistic children in this enlightened age? When Sparta thrived, the men took infants who seemed unwhole and left them on a mountainside where death came swiftly with a single bitter night or with the chance discovery by a hungry wolf or dog. Other cultures, closer to the present day, condoned the smashing of infant skulls against stones or trunks of trees when children were strange, worrisome, or unwanted.

Of course, the people of the United States abhor and reject such straightforward and efficient methods. They shield themselves from the guilt inherent in such outright acts of cruelty. They have constructed elaborate processes—rituals, if you will, in an anthropological sense— to protect their sensibilities from the pain of child killing and from the unpleasantness of inflicting ostracism (and all of the suffering and grief that goes with it) upon fellow citizens whose only crime is the misfortune to have borne and loved an autistic child.

How are these children killed? How are these parents ostracized? What rights are taken away from them? What things are they barred from doing that other citizens freely take for granted?

I will take these questions and by giving examples, citing cases, and sharing from my own experience as the father of one of these beautiful, outcast children, make case. My beginning statements are not fantasy but absolute chilling truth.

The execution of autistic children takes place in a slow and tedious fashion. It is done with such deftness and subtlety that in most cases the parents, and often those carrying out the death-dealing acts, are unaware that they are killing a child. They think that any number of things—mostly things spoken of in words that carry the connotation of caring, helping, healing—are taking place but certainly not the deliberate ending of a human life. But death comes. And the life is ended. And society is rid of yet another nuisance child.

I feel the tears now, growing in my chest for George, my adolescent autistic boy. The process is working slowly toward his end, and somewhere the cold eye of an unfeeling society is fixed upon him, and I am only one. What can I do?

To tell you how the killing is carried out so that you will understand it clearly, I must first tell you about the children who are marked. I want you to know who they are, how they came into life, where they live, what their characteristics are, and what kind of people their mothers and fathers are.

Who are they? They have names like everyone else. They are called George, Tommy, Andrea, Missy, Lorcan, Anthony, Frankie,

Wayne, Danny, Wally, Mike, Steve, Sara, and Melinda—almost any name you pick, there is an autistic child named that.

They came into life just the same as everyone else. They were conceived by men and women, most of whom loved each other; were married and committed to each other; wanted children in their homes to care for, to bring up, and educate in the ways of their families and cultures; wanted for them the same things that parents of other children want for their offspring—good lives, success in their endeavors, freedom to come and go in a free society, enough food to eat, clothes to wear, shelter from the cold, comfortable homes, good friends, good services when they are sick, strength to deal with the problems of life, pleasure in living, healthy children.

Autistic children are found throughout the world. They are born into families of all racial, ethnic, and social backgrounds (NSAC, 1977). No groups of people, by whatever criteria of discrimination, are safe from the possibility that some of their children will be autistic.

Part of the reason that these children are killed is that there are so few of them, they are so badly misunderstood, their parents are scattered and have little power to effect social change. Autism occurs in approximately 5 out of every 10,000 births and is four times more common in boys than girls. Since autism is so rare and occurs in every level of society, there can be—there is—no concentration of these children—or their parents—in any place, geographic or social, so that they can easily know each other, organize, come to grips with common problems and exert political pressure. In a town or county of 10,00 people, you can expect to have no more than 5 who are autistic, or, at the most, 10 parents of autistic children. In a city of 100,000 people, you can expect to have no more than 50 who are autistic, or, at the most, 100 parents of autistic children. In a state of 5,000,000 people, you can expect to have no more than 2,500 who are autistic, or, at the most, 5,000 parents of autistic children. In a nation of 200,000,000 people, you can expect to have no more than 100,000 who are autistic, or, at the most, 200,000 parents of autistic children.

The fact is that in towns or counties of 10,000 people it is most common for the leadership—political, social, medical, educational, or otherwise—to be totally unaware of autism or of the 5 autistic people who can statistically be expected to live among them. In cities of 100,000 people it is most common for only a few of the political, social, medical, educational, or other leaders or service providers to know of autism or to provide for autistic people, or to know personally even one of the 50 citizens who are autistic. In states of 5,000,000 people, or thereabout, it is most common for most of the leaders to know next to nothing and care even less about autism or the 2,500 autistic citizens who exist scattered about and invisible among the population. In the nation the same pattern exists, and the killing goes on unmercifully, while the leaders respond with the same sympathy to the cries of parents, to the agony of the condemned children, that the ocean gives to drowning men and women spilled into it from a sinking vessel.

Collectively, and in most cases, individually, the leaders—local, state, and national—don't care. They can't be bothered. They'd rather spend their time and energy in other ways, they'd rather spend the public money on other things, they don't have time to listen, they won't make the effort to understand, they don't think it is their job, they think it too much trouble to change. In short, they aren't concerned that autistic children are dying, that they, the leaders, are part of the killing process, that parents of autistic children are suffering, and that they, the leaders, are guiding the vast, unthinking machinery that, like a medieval torture rack, is inflicting that very suffering. The screams so rarely reach their ears. The tragedy so rarely touches their lives.

What are the characteristics of these condemned children and their parents? The parents have no characteristics different from those of other citizens. They are men and women like everyone else. They are good and bad, successes and failures, rich and poor (by the same ratio as others), intelligent and quick, dense and slow to learn. They work on farms and in cities, are professional people and laborers, black and white, Protestant, Catholic, Jewish, Islamic, etc. They are no more nor less insane than anyone else.

Perhaps it is not entirely correct to say that these parents have no characteristics that are different from those of other people. First, it is true that *before* they become parents of autistic children, they are no different. But afterwards, perhaps they become different.

Parents of autistic children have been known to do things or engage in behavior that obviously sets them apart from the norm. To begin with, they have the unmitigated gall to think that their children should be treated as human beings and not killed by society; that they should be educated according to their educational needs, just as other children are; that they should not be locked up in vast, malignant, concrete warehouses and stifled to death. They feel that they, as parents, should be helped to cope with the problems their children's condition produces; that they, as parents, need some time of their own away from the stress of dealing with autism; that they and their children should be free from the effects of social ostracism, professional ignorance, stupidity, and manipulation; and that they should not be taken advantage of, financially and emotionally, by rich doctors, psychologists, bureaucrats, quack researchers, and others who are padding their pocketbooks while engaging in the same kind of hocus-pocus that has enabled witch doctors, sorcerers, and other similar charlatans to rip off their fellow human beings while gaining riches and status for themselves since the beginning of time.

I know a beautiful woman who is in her sixties. She is as stable, intelligent, kind, caring, interested and interesting, vital and loving a woman as I have ever met. She is the mother of an autistic person, a man nearing forty. She and her son have been mistreated, malpracticed upon, legally stolen from, taken advantage of, denied services, denied rights, the object of verbal and physical abuse, and generally ignored or treated as fools by a small army of doctors, psychiatrists, bureaucrats, researchers, administrators, and other leaders in the various states in which she has lived.

Why? Because her son was autistic. None of it would have happened if her son had been born with the ability to function in the fashion that people call "normal." If he had, she would not have suffered in the manner that she has at the hands of those who have caused her pain. Her crime was that she did everything she knew how to do to help her son.

When the boy was very young, she noticed he was not developing as he should and that he was doing peculiar things such as screaming all night long, endlessly wriggling his fingers along the periphery of his vision, making funny little nonsense noises instead of talking, refusing to wear clothes, refusing to be comforted when upset, not looking people in the eye—all those sad and confounding, amusing, bittersweet and heart-rending little things that autistic children do in those early years. (Remember, parents? You remember. We remember. Doesn't it jolt tears into your eyes to remember? Doesn't it make you laugh and cry inside to look upon those strange and fearful days and see that beautiful child—yours—mine—in diapers, running aimlessly, laughing in the sunshine of a far-off, time-lost day, glimpsed fleetingly through the mist of long-gone years; amused at sounds unheard by us, at thoughts unknown, unknowable; terrified to lost, abandoned wailing at horrors unperceived and unperceivable to us—we who loved so long and painfully and unavailingly.)

So, with rising fear, she took the child to all the places from which help is said to come in our society—doctors, psychiatrists who probed with knowing smiles into the deepest personal regions of her life, specialists, treatment centers, hospitals, clinics. This went on and on through years of waiting rooms and corridors, through examinations, diagnostic tests, and lab reports, before a hundred polished desks, a hundred men in white until they both, she and her son, grew old and tired. (Remember, parents? Remember? For she is us and we are her.)

And what did the hundred (more or less, give or take a dozen or so, it doesn't matter) important, knowledgeable, people do?

They cleared their throats importantly.

They smoked their cigars and cigarettes casually.

They looked at her over smart bifocals wisely.

They wrote jargon in their secret files so knowledgeably.

They cruelly stamped a dozen labels on the child.

They sent her bills which she paid and paid and paid religiously.

They sent her away unaided and alone.

They did other things, too.

They held the struggling child down, drugged him senseless, and cut out part of his brain; they called it lobotomy, and she paid for it.

They tied him to a table, sent fierce jolts of electricity through the tender, already faulty, already damaged tissue inside his skull; they called it treatment, and she paid for it.

They said he was emotionally disturbed, they said she made him that way, they called her insulting names in a code language they made up themselves, to serve their own purposes. They said what they were doing was therapy, and she paid for it.

Finally, when the child had been reduced to a shuffling, drooling, brainless, hopeless creature who could not speak a single intelligible word, could not keep from soiling his pants with feces, could not attend to his simplest human needs, and was given to wild fits of self-destruction in a pathetic effort to rid himself of the burden of life, they took him away, tied him to a chair in a dreary, cold, and stinking ward in a crumbling, overcrowded "hospital." They called it care and she paid for it.

My God, isn't that enough? Oh, no, it isn't—not nearly enough. The bond between mother and child is strong. It is flesh caring for flesh, blood reaching out to blood, and does not end when institution doors clang harshly shut. My friend never stopped trying—she is trying now. She never stopped hoping—she is hoping now.

Sometimes when she drove 100 miles to visit her son, the staff at the institution sent her away. She asked them why, and they called her a nuisance. She wrote scores and scores of letters—asking, pleading, demanding, searching, cajoling to improve the conditions of his existence—and they said she interfered.

She saw him sitting, neglected, in his own feces and they rationalized this outrage. "We don't have the staff. . . . We do our best, but there isn't enough money. . . . The legislature won't. . . . The administration won't. . . . The rules won't . . . " and so on.

She learned that he was never taken out to walk in the sunlight. She saw his skin grow pale, his muscles wither from lack of use, his body sagging and old when it should have been young and strong, his broken mind untended, unstimulated, wasted.

Her conversations, condensed from a hundred meetings with administrators, directors, staff people, bureaucrats, "service providers," over the span of twenty years went something like this:

"Can you put him in a better ward?" "No." "Can you get him out to walk once a day?" "No." "He loves to swim. Can he swim sometimes?" "No." "Can you build a swimming pool? All the residents could use it. It would be good for them." "No." "Can you provide him some education, some training?" "No." "The community college is nearby. They will provide trainers if you will identify twelve people. Call it adult education and draft a program for them. Will you take the time?" "No." "The institution a mile away has a swimming pool. Can he go there once a week?" "No."

Once, in the 1960s, she escalated her simple requests into demands, drawing upon the strategy of black action groups. When she was rejected, she went in utter desperation—a lone, weary, aging woman—and lay her body in the street at the "hospital" where she caused a flurry of disruption until she was taken away.

Why, you might ask, did she not just take her son home, keep him there, and care for him herself? There are many reasons, not the least of which is that she did for years until her resources—financial, physical, and emotional—were drained.

Another is that she believed the myths, expounded by professionals, that somewhere in their heads, hidden in their books, behind some closed and secret doors beyond her knowing, was help and hope and care—if only she would trust and lay her burdens in their hands. She did, and they killed her son.

There is no pleasant ending to this story. There cannot be. A living corpse still rocks behind closed doors. A good and loving mother tends her wounds and keeps on trying.

The ritualistic killing of autistic children is a fascinating process to observe—if you can keep from being fooled by the subtle intricacies of it, or being consumed with rage at the cruelty of it, or being lulled into uncaring by the tedious slowness of it. One must be quite alert to even know that it is happening. Often death itself is the only clue that lets the nonparent know.

"Autistic Boy Found Dead in Mud Near Hospital," was the caption of a newspaper story one day in November. The story read somewhat like this:

" 'Death was due to exposure,' according to_____,the deputy state medical examiner, who added that further tests are scheduled to determine how long the boy had been dead.

"Hospital officials noticed that he was missing about four o'clock Wednesday afternoon, and, together with state police, searched for him until Friday.

"The governor learned of the missing boy Saturday and ordered several hundred state troopers and National Guard reservists to join the search. They were aided by state police helicopters and citizen band radio operators. . . .

"His body was found about noon Monday in a muddy area one mile east of the hospital grounds. He apparently had fallen into the mud and could not get out, police said."

The paper carried a photograph of a beautiful, thirteen-year-old, dark-eyed boy with bangs that hung low over his forehead and a wistful, faraway look on his soft features. "Footprints found Saturday near the hospital indicated_____ may have been alive then, despite the 20-degree temperatures during the nights he spent outside the hospital."

How could this be called a killing? Wasn't this just an accident? Didn't everybody show concern? Didn't they do all they could? Didn't the governor call out the National Guard? What justification do you have for those harsh and blaming words? Look deeper. There is more. It becomes apparent:

1. The state in which this occurred had no mandatory education law for the handicapped. They didn't care.
2. Even though the Education for all Handicapped Children Act (Public Law 94–142) was passed in 1975, there was no free, appropriate, public education available for the boy in the community where he lived. They didn't provide.
3. Even though the Congress of the United States passed Section 504 of the Rehabilitation Act of 1973, the anti-discrimination, civil rights act for the handicapped, this autistic child was closed out of services, closed out of education, closed out of programs provided for others—harshly discriminated against because of his handicap. They broke the law.
4. Even though landmark court cases handed down in 1972 declared that it is unconstitutional to provide education to others while leaving the handicapped unserved, autistic children continued to be denied. They ignored the courts.

Here is the final, heartbreaking irony: In a fit of compassion, when death was already at hand, when the process had reached the ragged edge of its conclusion, the government, the governor, the administration of that hospital, of that state, spent something in the neighborhood of $40,000 in five days to find that pitiful body that they had rendered lifeless by their inaction, by their lawlessness, by their refusal to care, by their discrimination, by their denial of rights, by their inhuman stupidity.

You figure it: Five days of searching by 200 people at 10 hours a day at a round figure of $4 an hour. That's not counting the helicopter, the automobiles, the gasoline, the CB radios, the wear and tear, the laundry bills from slogging around in the woods, the telephone calls, the rescue equipment, the secretary's time, the medical examiner's time, the lab reports, etc. Forty-thousand dollars! That would have provided one condemned autistic child with five to eight years of individualized education designed to meet his needs, to help him grow, to relieve his parents of the burden of autism for six or seven hours a day, to save them from suffering, to keep him in the safety of his home, to grant him life in our society.

What are the characteristics of these children that people in the United States are getting rid of in the manner described above? First of all, they have something wrong with their brains. Their brains don't work like other people's brains allegedly do. It is a physical something. Here, with interspersed comments about my son and other autistic children, is what the National Society for Autistic Children says about autism in its official "Short Definition," adopted in Orlando, Florida, June 27, 1977:

Autism is a severely incapacitating life-long developmental disability which typically appears during the first three years of life.

A harried mother, her face drawn with fatigue, large blue circles under her eyes from sleepless nights, her hair unkempt, her clothes disheveled, struggles to keep a beautiful, curly-haired child of eighteen months or so on her lap. The child is moving constantly, crawling, reaching, pulling, never still, fretting, making funny noises, going over her shoulder, leaning backward off of her lap, pulling at her dress, going, going. She is in a pediatrician's office and she is speaking, "Doctor, I am afraid something is wrong with George."

The doctor smiles. "He's certainly an active little boy. What seems to be the trouble?"

"He won't sleep. He jumps in his crib all the time, up and down, up and down. He has already torn one crib apart jumping. And he has these tantrums. I don't know what starts them. I can't seem to do anything about them. He screams. I know the neighbors think I am killing him. And it goes on, sometimes all night and all day. He won't let me hold him. And neither my husband nor I can comfort him when he is like that." There are tears in her eyes now, and she tries not to sob. The little boy has pulled the shoulder strap of her dress down. She moves to fix that, while the child wriggles away under her arm. She catches him by the leg and pulls him back onto her lap.

"I've examined him carefully, and I can tell you he is a healthy little boy."

"But why does he do this? Why does he scream all night long—sometimes twenty-four hours a day?"

"Twenty-four hours a day?" The doctor lowers his head, smiles slightly, and looks at the woman out of the corners of his eyes.

"Yes. I can't stand it. I am so tired I can hardly move, but I can't sleep. I am afraid if I go to sleep he will get out of the house at night in the dark, and I won't be able to find him in time." She is crying harder now, and her cheeks are wet with tears. Her body is shaking, and she bites her lips.

"Now, now. You are upset. Let me give you something to help you rest. When you have rested, you will feel better. All children have tantrums from time to time. Just ignore them, and they will go away. You've got a very healthy little boy." He writes out a prescription. The boy slips between his mother's knees, hands reaching for the floor. She catches him by the hips and wearily hauls him again into her lap. He seems to be smiling at something invisible in the upper corners of the room.

"Let me know if it helps," the doctor says kindly.

"All right," she says, taking the slip of paper. She struggles to hold the child as she walks toward the door.

In the outer office the receptionist says, "That will be $10."

The symptoms of autism are caused by a physical disorder of the brain and include

1. Disturbances in the rate of appearance of physical, social, and language skills.

In a small development house on the outskirts of a city of 60,000, a little boy stands on a chair and flicks an electric light switch on and off.

"Light, light," he says, laughing. "Light, light, light." His father and mother beam. "Yes, George, that's a light. Good boy! George can turn on the light!"

"Light, light," says the child, laughing as if to himself.

Fourteen years have passed. It is another town and another place. A young man, his curly hair turned brown, and a little fuzz beginning to grow upon his upper lip, runs to his father who is walking toward him along a gravel path. He gives a funny little jump as he runs and laughs.

"Hey, George! Have you been a good boy today?"

The young man comes to his father, throws one arm around his neck while hiding his face with his other arm. He moves his face close to his father's. He takes his arm away and looks into his father's eyes. He has a searching, almost wistful look, and his voice is plaintive, questioning, urgent as he says, "Light. Light." Pause. "Light, light, light?"

His father looks at him quietly and puts his arms about the boy and holds him tight. He looks off into the treetops where the sky is soft blue and flecked with clouds, and he bites his lip until it hurts.

2. *Abnormal responses to sensations. Any one or a combination of sight, hearing, touch, pain, balance, smell, taste, and the way a child holds his body are affected.*

Pain. It is winter, and a freezing, sleet-filled rain has been falling heavily since dawn. Even inside where the heat is turned high the cold can be felt coming through the walls and window glass and doors.

It is quiet in the house, and a woman looks up from her work in the kitchen suddenly, as if she has been nudged. "Frank, where is George?"

The man is in the back of the house.

"What?" he says, raising his voice to be heard.

"Do you see George?"

"No," says the man, "I thought he was with you."

"Oh, my God. He is outside again."

And he is. Standing barefoot on the frozen lawn, the little boy of three is drenched to the skin; the cold rain is running off his clothes and down his neck and along his legs and arms. He is smiling absently as he picks tiny ice-rimmed buds, one at a time, from a camelia bush.

Rubbed down, dry, and warm again, he tries the bolted doors and presses his face against the windows to find his bush and frozen buds.

Balance. It is summer. A neighbor has propped a ladder against the side of his house, and is carefully removing pine straw and leaves from the gutters along the edge of his roof. Suddenly there is a yell.

"George! Get down from there! Frank! George is on the roof!"

A little boy in training pants trots merrily from one end of the ranch-style house to the other along the roof line, stands confidently with his toes curled over the far edge, looks down, tosses a stick, watches it fall to the ground, turns, repeats the route, and does the same thing at the other end. The neighbor, with a frozen look of fear upon his face, looks on in horror and amazement.

After coming to the scene, the boy's father looks up and yells: "George! Get down! You come down this minute!" The boy appears not to notice. "I'm getting a switch!" The father picks up a stick from the yard and holds it up. "You come down here right now!"

The boy gives his father a quick glance. He sees the switch and scampers to the ladder. In a moment he is on the ground and running toward his house.

"Whew! I thought he was going to fall and break his neck," says the neighbor, relaxing.

"Well. I know that was scarey. But I didn't think he would fall. The other day I saw him walking along the top of the fence, just like a tightrope walker, holding out his hands to balance. He walked all the way around the yard and never fell. And once, last year, he climbed on top of his swing set and did the same thing. It's amazing. I guess we'd better move the ladder."

3. *Speech or language are absent or delayed, while specific think-ing capabilities may be present. Immature rhythms of speech, limited understanding of ideas, and the use of words without attaching the usual meaning to them is common.*

A child of seven is in a special classroom at a university. He reaches for a button-sized, sugar-coated chocolate on the table in front of him. A man on the other side of the table pulls it away. The child's parents watch from behind a one-way mirror in another room. "Say 'candy,' George. This is candy. Candy. You want the candy. Say 'candy' and you can have it." The man holds the candy near the child's face. The child reaches for it again, and again it is pulled away. "Candy, George. Candy. Say 'candy' and you can have it."

This goes on and on. The boy squirms. He gets up and runs around the room. He is carried back. He reaches again and again. But always the candy is pulled away. At last, after what seems hours, the child looks at the man. "Ca-gn," he says, almost inaudibly.

"Good! Good, George!" The man thrusts the candy into the child's mouth. He touches him and rubs his back. "Good talking! Good saying 'candy!' Good boy! Good boy!"

Behind the glass screen the parents smile and squeeze each other's hands. "He said it! He said it! He can talk! It works!"

4. *Abnormal ways of relating to people, objects and events. Autistic children do not respond appropriately to adults and other children. Objects and toys are not used as normally intended.*

It is Sunday. A hymn is being played softly on the organ. At the front of the church men and women kneel, heads bowed, hands cupped. A priest bends toward them, one at a time, intoning: "This is my body which is given for thee. . . . "

From the pews there is a flurry of motion. A small figure in short pants darts into the aisle, his bare legs pumping.

"Take and eat this in remembrance that Christ died for thee. . . ."

The small figure has reached the kneeling communicants now, and he wriggles in between them, pushing with his hands, ducking his head beneath the altar rail. While this goes on, his father is in hot pursuit.

". . . and live on Him by faith . . . ," says the priest.

The boy is at the altar now. His father is opening the altar rail. An acolyte, a young man who knows the boy, is reaching for him. The boy's feet are scrambling at the front of the altar; one hand is pulling him onto it, his other hand is reaching for the Eucharistic candle. Already he is blowing, "whoosh, whoosh," and the candle flickers. The acolyte scoops him up and hands him, struggling, to his father who quickly ducks out of the sanctuary with the boy in his arms.

". . . and live on Him by faith—and thanksgiving."

Autism occurs by itself or in association with other disorders which affect the function of the brain such as viral infections, metabolic disturbances, and epilepsy. On IQ testing, approximately 60 percent have scores below 50, 20 percent between 50 and 70, and only 20 percent greater than 70. Most show wide variations of performance on different tests and at different times.

When David was three years old, he screamed for hours, had no language, sometimes tried to hurt himself, ranked 50 on an IQ test. It was the same with Clyde.

David's parents found some aberrant professionals who encouraged them to keep him at home, helped them to work with him each day using an especially designed program to improve his behavior, strengthen his abilities, increase his social skills, capitalize on his strengths. Clyde went into an institution "for his own good and to protect his family" where he learned to rock and spin and bang his head.

When David was seven, he was in regular kindergarten, playing with other children, learning new things. Tests showed David's IQ at 100. When Clyde was eleven, he was still in an institution, still rocking and spinning—though with much more finesse—and tests showed Clyde's IQ at 40 or below. A leather helmet protected his head.

When David was fourteen, he was in junior high school. In the summer he mowed grass for pocket money and had a part in a summer play. When Clyde was fourteen, he strangled to death on some food when the attendants weren't looking.

It cost the state $144,000 to protect Clyde and his family for nine years. During that time some important doctors made lots of money which they spent and helped the economy.

It cost the state $18,000 to help David and his family for nine years. David is one of the few autistic children who is going to make it. He will earn enough money to pay his taxes, buy the things he needs, and help the economy. Not many important doctors have or shall benefit.

Autistic people live (or can, or ought, or deserve to live) a normal life span. Since symptoms change, and some may disappear with age, periodic reevaluations are necessary to respond to changing needs. Special education programs using behavioral methods and designed for specific individuals have proven most helpful.

David got it and lived. Clyde did not, and he died.

Supportive counseling may be helpful for families with autistic members, as it is for families who have members with other severe life-long disabilities.

A pleasant room sits off a tile corridor at a famous university medical school. In it is a bookcase filled with heavy, hard-backed books, a number of important journals, and a few professional magazines. Impressionist prints, expensively framed, are placed tastefully on the walls. In front of the bookcase stands a polished wooden desk with a glass top decorated with still more books, a calendar, a small file for addresses and phone numbers, a letter opener, and an ash tray which holds the remains of an expensive cigar. In front of the desk and to one side is a table with a lamp, still more magazines, and another ash tray. A comfortable stuffed chair, not overly large, sits next to the table. A woman who is visibly exhausted sits uneasily in the chair, her pocketbook on her lap, looking at a psychiatrist who sits behind the desk asking her questions and writing things unobtrusively on a yellow pad.

"Why were you afraid to make your appointment yesterday?" he asks in a professional voice. "I wasn't afraid, I was sick." "You felt sick?" "I was sick." "How were you sick?" "I began to get sick on the way up," she says. "Hmmmm." "When I got here night before last, I was very sick, and I simply could not come in yesterday. My husband came and brought George." "Yes, I know, but I can't help you if you won't come to your appointments." "But I couldn't help it if I became sick. I think it is the flu." The psychiatrist smiles benignly and lights his cigar. He writes something down. "Don't you believe that I was sick?" "Why do you think I don't believe you?"

"You don't act as though you believe me. I was up all night sick at my stomach. My head was killing me. I had a fever. I am still sick today. I would have come if I could have gotten out of bed. Besides, I don't understand what we are doing. Don't you want George here? Don't you want to see him? We have been coming here, driving one hundred miles both ways, for nearly two years. Can't you help George? He just runs around in the halls with one or the other of us following him while you talk to one of us. I don't see how that is helping him. We need to know what is the matter with George. We need to know what to do to help him."

"We want to help him, but we can't unless we talk to you, and when you break your appointments. . . ." "But I told you I was sick, and I am sorry that I was, but I couldn't help it." "Mmmm," says the psychiatrist, and makes more notes.

Later, on the long drive home, the woman, hot with fever, speaks to her husband. "I don't know why we keep coming up here. Dr._____doesn't believe anything I say. He keeps trying to make me say things that aren't true. He is not telling us what we can do about George. He doesn't even want to see George. I don't know why we keep coming up here."

Her husband is silent for a while. George is rocking quietly in the back seat. The engine hums. Cars pass. Finally he speaks:

"I don't know what else we can do. Those schools for children like George cost $10,000 a year, and that's more than I make—God knows it costs enough to come here. If it's an emotional thing, maybe he can find out how to get him over it. I suppose he is trying to help us. The only other thing is an institution, and we will never do that."

"No," says the wife. "We are never going to do that to George, not ever." And she turns and looks at the little boy, gently touches his damp curls. "Oh, George," she says, softly. "Why can't you tell us what's the matter?"

The severe form of the syndrome may include the most extreme forms of self-injurious, repetitive, highly unusual, and aggressive behaviors. Such behaviors may be persistent and highly resistant to change, often requiring unique management, treatment, or teaching techniques.

It is Saturday, and a man is mowing the grass in the front yard of a small suburban home. A child about four wearing a tee shirt and short pants is walking aimlessly about, wriggling his fingers oddly near his face and making sounds with his mouth that sound like "pop-wheeew! pop-wheeew! pop-wheeew!"

The man and the lawn mower disappear around the corner of the house, following the edge of an expanding corridor of neatly cut grass. In a moment they return, following the widening corridor, and the child is gone. The man stops, looks around, bends down and turns off the lawn mower.

"George!" No answer. "George!" No answer. "George, where are you?" Still no answer.

He runs to the house, leans inside the door, and asks his wife, who is sewing in the living room, "Did George come in?" "No." "Well, he is gone." "Frank, he has been trying to sniff gas all day. I bet I pulled him away from the neighbor's garage fourteen times before you came home." "Sniffing gas again! I thought we had all the gas put away where he couldn't get it." "He's learned how to get the lid off David's lawn mower." "Oh."

He turns from the door, already running, and lopes across the lawn, beside a flower bed, through a gate in the fence, across the neighbor's yard, and as he nears the garage he sees the door to the tool shed ajar, and two small feet, their soles black from not wearing shoes, sticking out.

"George, get out of there right now." There is no response. Flinging open the door, he finds the child on his knees, his arms wrapped around the mower and his nose and mouth pressed into the open gasoline tank. He is taking deep breaths.

The man takes the child into his arms. The smell of gasoline is strong on the boy's breath, his eyes are glazed, and he is near unconsciousness.

Later, in the night, as the child rocks quietly in a tiny wooden rocking chair which he is scooting with the motions of his body along a darkened hallway near his parents' room, the man and his wife discuss the happenings of the day.

"How many times did you put him to bed?" the man asks. "He is up and rocking again."

"I don't know. Eight or ten times. He will go to sleep when he is ready. You know he rocks all night. Did you lock the doors?"

"Yes."

"What are we going to do about his sniffing gas? He almost knocked himself out today."

"Well, you know what the psychiatrists told us."

"I don't think they know what they are talking about. They don't believe me when I tell them how many times he runs away. And they want us to go get him each time, never lose our temper, take him by the hand, and bring him gently home."

"How many times did you get him back from David's house today?" the man asks.

"I know it must have been every fifteen or twenty minutes. I couldn't get a thing done until you came home. Frank, I can't keep this up."

"I was running after him all afternoon. I think he needs a good switching when he does that. We just can't let him sniff gas."

"You know what they say about switching," replies the wife.

The next day George searches for gasoline all through the morning and into the afternoon. Each time he is brought gently home by his parents who try to divert his attention. They tickle him and roll with him on the grass. They swing him on his swing set. They play with him in the sand pile. They give him a hose and a bucket of water. Nothing works. Finally his father gives way to his natural instincts. "Damn it," he says to himself, "those people are fools." He cuts a switch with his pocketknife as he watches the little boy trotting away to the neighbor's garage. As the child twists the lid from the lawn mower tank, he catches him.

"No! No! No! No sniffing gas! You will not sniff gas!" He applies the switch hard to the little boy's bare legs as the child flees for home.

The next time George heads for the neighbor's garage, he looks back over his shoulder. "No," says his father, reaching for the switch and showing it to the child. The boy stops at the fence. Gas sniffing is over.

In another state, another couple is faced with a horrifying problem. Their son, whom we will call Larry, cuts himself with broken glass in order to smear the bright red blood on the walls of his room.

He has done it again and again with determination that confounds his parents. They are using plastic cups, dishes, and glasses, but still the child finds something with a cutting edge, something he can smash and press into the flesh of his hands and arms to get blood. His hands are covered with scars. The walls of his room have been painted again and again to cover the stains. It is a daily, desperate, frustrating effort to keep the child from cutting himself and smearing his blood. When the slashes are deep and require stiches, he pulls them out. He opens the wounds with his fingers and finds the blood again.

What did the professionals offer this couple and their child? Talk. Jargon. Analysis. Tests. Play therapy. Institutionalization. Physical restraint. Nothing. Some children have been tied to their institutional beds, their hands and arms wrapped tightly against their bodies, their feet and legs bound. Some have remained like that for years. More than a few have died.

But these people would not have that. Driven by their care for their son, they searched for a better way. They found it. They had to do it alone without professional help, against professional advice.

One day the mother read an article in a professional journal about an unusual method of teaching self-destructive children to stop doing violent things to themselves. It was a method used in research, and the results had been dramatic.

She showed the article to her doctors. They would have nothing to do with it. So, in desperation, she and her husband made up their minds to undertake the procedure on their own.

She bought a cattle prod at a hardware store. A cattle prod is a heavy instrument, like a short baton or a policeman's billy club. It is filled with batteries. It has a handle on one end, and at the other end are two short, blunt pieces of metal. When the prod is turned on and the two metal nipples are pressed against an object, an electrical circuit is created. It shocks the object. If you press it against your arm, the sensation is immediate and highly unpleasant. If you press it where the skin is close to the bone, the pain will linger for a few minutes. If you press it against your flesh, the shock will cease immediately upon removal. It does not burn or bruise, but you do not want it to happen again.

To use a thing like this on a child, for whatever reason, is a desperate, last-ditch measure. In this case, the alternatives are few and grim: The child cuts and cuts himself. Finally he does it and is not found until he has bled to death in his bed. Or he is locked up in an institution and dies there, cut off from life, bound up or drugged senseless, or both.

Here is the scene: The child, his mother and father are together in the basement of their home. There is a glass ashtray on the concrete floor. As the parents watch, the child darts to the ashtray, picks it up, and smashes it on the concrete. He quickly sits down beside the broken pieces and begins to press his right hand upon the jagged edges, straightening his arm, leaning his body weight upon it.

His mother turns on the prod. "No!" she says. There is a slight buzzing sound. She touches his forearm with the metal tips.

"Uuuuuh! Uuuuuuuh!" cries the child, and he leaps up, a look of fear and amazement upon his face. He runs about the room, holding his arm. His parents stand back.

Presently the child returns to the broken ashtray. He glances at his parents and begins again to cut himself.

"No! No!" shouts his mother. She produces the prod. This time the child sees it and darts away.

"Hold him," says his mother.

The father seizes the child. There is a struggle. The boy is large and strong. He sees the prod and he is frightened.

"Uuuuuunh! Uuuuuuunh!" he cries in terror.

The mother is trembling now, as she comes to him with the prod. She knows how it feels. She has tried it upon herself.

"Hold him," she says quietly.

The father and the boy are on the floor. The boy is kicking and fighting to get away, his eyes riveted on the prod.

"UUUUUUUUUU—UUUUUUUUUNH!" he cries. "UUUUUUU— UUUUUUNH!"

"No! No! Larry. No Cutting! No cutting!" she says in a loud voice. There are tears in her eyes. She seizes the boy's forearm and presses the prod against it, holding it there, feeling the electricity passing into her own body.

This time the shock is long, and the child screams and screams with pain. When it is done, the boy flees to his room, and the parents stand there looking at each other. The man puts his arms around his wife and holds her as she weeps.

Their program for using the prod is a simple one. Cutting *always* produces a shock. Otherwise, the prod is kept out of sight. The cutting ceased.

No known factors in the psychological environment of a child have been shown to cause autism.

Do you hear that out there, Bruno Bettleheim[1]? Do you hear? Are we getting through to you? We said: *No known factors in the psychological environment of a child have been shown to cause autism.* Now do you hear? Do you understand?

That means we didn't do it, Bruno. We've known that all along. It means that careful, objective, scientific people have carried out study after study, test after test, interview after interview; and have written paper after paper in journal after journal which show that we, the parents of autistic children, are just ordinary people. Not any crazier than others. Not "refrigerator parents" any more than others. Not cold intellectuals any more than others. Not neurotic or psychopathic or sociopathic or any of those words that have been made up.

It means, Dr. Bettleheim, that you, and all those others like you who have been laying this incredible guilt trip on us for over twenty years, you are wrong and ought to be ashamed of yourselves.

---

[1]Bettleheim contends that some parental attitudes, feelings, and child-rearing practices expose a child to such extreme stress that he responds by severe withdrawal, characterized as autism. He recommends that the child be institutionalized so that institutional staff may replace the parents (hence, "parentectomy") and effectively treat the child in a less primitive ("feral," like wild animals, wolves) environment. See the chapter reference list.

"Feral mothers" indeed! You are a feral mother, Bruno. Take that and live with it for a while. It doesn't feel very good, does it?

And "parentectomy"? It is my considered professional opinion, after having carefully examined all of the facts, that nothing short of a Bruno-ectomy will improve conditions in this case. And a Freud-ectomy. And a psychiatrist-ectomy. And a jargon-ectomy. And a professional baloney-ectomy.

It is further indicated by the facts in this case, that an abject public apology is called for by all that horde of ignorant physicians, smug psychiatrists, know-it-all social workers, inept educators, clap-trap therapists—all the people who have assembled wealth and status for themselves by taking advantage of our suffering and the suffering of our innocent children.

Don't worry. We won't spit in your eye and tell you to go to hell—a treatment you so richly deserve. Just tell us you are sorry, that you will try to do better. It's not hard. You know you need to do it. We will accept. We will say: "That's all right. It's all over, now. It was a bad scene, but we are ready to forget it."

"Here. Let's shake. Take our hands. We need you. God knows we need you to help us bring some sensitivity into this world for the sake of our children who are absolutely going to be killed if it does not come."

And here is the hard part, friends. We don't really expect you to respond. The system works for you too well—no matter if it grieves us and kills our children. Your professional structure is too strong—no matter if it is built on myths and lies and held together with trickery and mystique. Your status is too self-satisfying. The money, friends, is much too good. And so it goes.

I'm sorry, George. We are all so very sorry.

References

Bettleheim, B. *Love is not enough.* Glencoe, New York: Free Press, 1950.

Bettleheim, B. *The empty fortress: Infantile autism and the birth of the self.* London: Collier-Macmillan, 1967.

Dussault, W. Speech presented at the meeting of the National Society for Autistic Children, Orlando, July 1977.

Mills v. Board of Education of the District of Columbia, 348 F. Supp. 866 (D.D.C. 1972).

National Society for Autistic Children, Board of Directors and Professional Advisory Board. *A short definition of autism.* Albany: Authors, 1977.

P.L. 94–142, The Education for All Handicapped Children Act.

P.L. 93–112, as amended by P.L. 93–51, enacting Section 504, Rehabilitation Act of 1973.

James J. Gallagher
Gertrude C. Gallagher

James J. Gallagher is Kenan professor of education and the director of the Frank Porter Graham Child Development Center, University of North Carolina at Chapel Hill, former deputy assistant secretary for Planning, Research, and Evaluation, U.S. Office for Education, and former associate commissioner of Education and chief of the Bureau of Education for the Handicapped.

Gertrude G. [Rani] Gallagher is a graduate of New Haven State Teachers College and has done graduate work at New York University. She taught at Southberry Training School, a mental retardation center in Connecticut.

Family Adaptation to a Handicapped Child and Assorted Professionals

Some years ago the senior author of this paper had occasion to write an article entitled "Rejecting Parents?" (Gallagher, 1956). In that article he took professionals to task for reaching a too-easy conclusion that parents tend to reject their handicapped children. Too many professionals seemed to put down parents when, in fact, the parents needed their sympathy and support. He comments as follows:

> Needless to say, every parent can be indicted at one time or another if expression of negative values is the only criterion for parental rejection, especially if the observer happens to catch the parent under conditions of stress. When we think of the problems that parents of normal children face and then consider the extra stress which is placed on parents of handicapped children, it is little wonder that the term used loosely could apply to almost any mother or father. What parent could be completely happy or positively oriented to a child who is quadriplegic, or blind, or severely mentally retarded, or, for that matter, completely normal in every respect? (Gallagher, 1956, p. 273)

The Problem

In the next year, our second son was born, and we were soon to live through some of the problems and issues that were discussed professionally in that article. Our son, unlike his healthy older brother, seemed to have continuing illnesses in infancy and as a toddler. These illnesses were variously called bronchitis, pneumonia, or just plain flu. Although a diagnosis was made early of bronchial asthma, like most parents who have little or no knowledge of such special health problems, the full significance of that diagnosis did not dawn upon us until much later.

The next ten years were a mixture of periodic acute crises appearing against a backdrop of general normal development. This, of course, is quite different from the parent of the severely handicapped child and creates very different parental problems. Our child's intellectual level has not been affected nor his ability to form a reasonable relationship with other youngsters and within his own family. His school performance remained good despite his frequent absences and no one really thought of him as handicapped.

Our son had a hidden disorder, one that could not be seen or appreciated until it went into its acute phase. He must have been hospitalized a hundred times during that twelve-year period. We have had intimate contacts with countless emergency rooms, oxygen tents, and interns taking case histories—the same case history over and over again. Our child would progress, in a terrifyingly rapid succession, from wheezing, to gasping for breath, to absolute helplessness, and finally to a coma unless treatment was provided with dispatch and decisiveness.

These attacks often struck with the suddenness of a thunderstorm, seemingly coming out of nowhere and suddenly being upon us. One of the chronic parental fears was that this thunderstorm would strike at a time and a place where there would be no shelter, that is, no competent professionals around to help us with this problem. The thought of being caught on a highway late at night between towns or in a strange city with no known resources or guide as to where to go is a constant companion of parents of chronically asthmatic children.

One of the ways such a handicap changes the life of the family is that it brings the young family face to face with the prospects of death at a time when most families are filled with enthusiasm and energy, and in which the prospect of death touching that family is fleetingly encountered. To see one's preschool child in a coma in an oxygen tent struggling for breath is sobering, and the prospect that the child will never reach maturity was one that had to be considered.

The Search for Help

One of the major problems of all parents of handicapped children is finding someone who really knows what this condition is all about and what to do about it. We lived in a university community, but it did not have a medical school. While that community had hard-working and well-meaning pediatricians and other medical specialists, they had rarely seen a case of this severity and really didn't know what to do. We were referred to a specialist in Chicago after local treatments had failed, and Sean and his mother made a trip for desensitization treatments every few weeks by train, the first of many futile attempts to apply some kind of rational long-range treatment program.

We were one of the first families to experience the era of cortisone. We were told (after several years of treatments that didn't work, or almost worked, or worked sometimes, but not others) that there was a powerful drug that had promise of helping asthmatic children. The trouble was, as the doctors pointed out, it was also powerful enough to have many unfavorable side effects, and it should be taken only when absolutely necessary. We weren't clear at first, and the doctors were rather vague themselves, about what these horrors were. It was clear that a balancing act was required between lowering the dosage and risking an attack of asthma, and increasing the dosage in such a way as to have him clear of asthmatic attacks but possibly suffering some other side effect. We as parents had to wonder whether in providing for our own security (freedom from attacks), we weren't harming our child in another way.

Professionals and Parents

Since both of us were trained to work with children ourselves, our relationships with professionals had a special set of qualities and difficulties about them. The anxieties and concerns of parents are such that they often want to credit more expertise and capabilities to the professionals than they, in fact, possess. As parents we would have very much liked to believe in the invincibility and complete mastery of the professionals with whom we came in contact. Our sense of our own limitations and the limitations of our own professions prevented us from doing that. We particularly had warning flags thrown up when we ran across a professional who maintained the fiction that we had come to the source of all knowledge that would straighten out all our problems and all we had to do was to leave everything in his hands. Nor did it help, in reading the literature on the subject, to realize that the treatment programs rested upon some extraordinarily inadequate and poorly done research.

Our continuous contact with the medical profession from the late fifties through the early seventies allowed us to see many changes taking place in the delivery of health services, practically all of them for the better for parents. Even in the earlier time periods, we were pleased to find an understanding of how important it was for parents to stay with young children in the hospital. This was most important psychologically, since most young children are terribly uncertain in a strange hospital and surrounded entirely by strangers. The notion that their parents may go and never return, or that they will never see their parents again, is an irrational but not unusual response in the youngster of five or six years of age. It seemed to us that the growing understanding of child development in the medical profession was reflected by the policies that allowed us to remain in important contact with our son in the hospital.

One of the special problems that we became aware of, only in retrospect, was that our son was an amazingly good patient. He instantly became the favorite in practically any emergency room or hospital where he had to stay. He did this through the process of being in good spirits and good humor, bearing stoically his problems, and never complaining about any treatment or shot that he received. In many respects he behaved as the model patient. What we only slowly began to realize is that his model patient behavior stemmed from his fear that he was going to die, hence his complete willingness to bear anything to prevent that.

It is impossible for us to understand the emotions and feelings of a child who finds himself suddenly unable to breathe. He can see that those adults who are ordinarily capable, his parents, can do nothing but transport him to where he can get help. Our belated insight about his fears convinced us that any youngster in similar situations should have extended counseling and discussions with professionals about such terrors, which are almost certain to be there.

One of the disturbing aspects of dealing with the professionals is that when one is playing the role of parent, one is automatically stripped of any knowledge or expertise that one might otherwise possess. Even simple parent observations are suspect because of the possibility of "bias." Over a period of ten years we both became quite expert in our ability to identify the onset of an attack and to predict the course of that attack. On many occasions, we tried, more or less desperately, to share those predictions with physicians with whom we had come in contact on an emergency basis. We almost uniformly found our judgments to be discounted.

For example, we became aware of the medical strategy of choosing the least intrusive treatment and seeing if it will work. If it doesn't work, then try the next most intrusive effort or drug and continue in this way until one finds the level of treatment necessary to achieve the desired results. This is fine for the ordinary patient. Whenever doctors adopted this routine strategy, we often found our son in the midst of a severe attack before the level or strength of medication could be applied that could prevent it. On numerous occasions we tried to point out to the doctor that our son goes into attacks sharply and severely in almost a toboggan-slide style. Unless one could catch him before the toboggan had a chance to gain momentum, he would be in the midst of a severe attack before anything could be done.

Much to our frustration, we watched our son go into such attacks as the doctors ignored our comments and proceeded in a plodding fashion to apply slightly stronger and stronger medication as the last medication failed. All too often we had to observe our youngster in the midst of a severe attack. Fortunately for us, those physicians with whom we became acquainted over an extended period of time formed a relationship of trust with us which allowed us to work as a team. Then our own observations and years of experience were brought to bear on the situation in a constructive fashion. It certainly came home to us how easy it is for the professional to ignore parents' expressions of feelings or observations or intuitive judgments as to what might be the best course of action.

Professionals vs. the Parents

One of the unfortunate components of the era in which our child was growing up was that one of the predominant theories about bronchial asthma was that the parents could be the cause of the condition, rather than being part of the victims of it. We spent many hours being interviewed and questioned, with the obvious purpose of seeing if we were, in some fashion, precipitating the attacks of our child through our own anxieties and problems. Since we, in our other roles, were used to interviewing people, it was transparent in many cases what the intent of the questioning was, but that did not make it any less frustrating.

It is obvious that the parents are under tension when they have a handicapped child or a child who is subject to acute illnesses. Our feeling, which remains constant to this day, is that to accuse parents of creating the problem, whether the problem is asthma or autism or whatever, is akin to accusing the thunder of causing the storm. Our own tensions were clearly evident, though we tried to be *casual* upon hearing our child begin to wheeze, which signified the onset of an attack. We probably did contribute somewhat to the intensity of the attack, but that is quite different from being held responsible for the basic condition in the first place.

Such an attitude of "blame the parent," which was not uncommon among the professionals at that time, did create a distance in the relationship between the parents and the professionals and probably caused other unfavorable consequences as well. The parents of asthmatic children can develop an extraordinary sensitivity toward hearing the signs of an attack. We believed that we could hear our son wheezing from a distance of one hundred yards, and certainly there was no corner of the house where we could not be aware of his change of breathing pattern in his bedroom. At the same time, being aware that parents were thought to be a contributing factor often made us reluctant to seek immediate medical help on the grounds that we might be overreacting to the child's problems. This sometimes caused us to delay seeking medical help until the condition had gone too far. It caused a certain amount of wariness in our attitude and relationships toward the professionals. We weighed our statements to them, knowing that some poorly chosen word might cause them to charge off on this ill-conceived hypothesis.

One serious conflict between us as parents and the professionals came when Sean was in a hospital where the philosophy was clearly held that the parents were a contributing factor to the problem. When the physician in charge suggested at one time that we involve our youngster in an experiment to see if it were his fears, and our fears, that were essentially causing the seizures, we agreed. The cortisone treatment was removed and replaced with a placebo, so that Sean would still believe he was receiving cortisone. We would then see if he could be kept free of seizures by his mere belief that he was receiving the treatment that was supposed to be helping him.

Unfortunately, the result of such an experiment was that within twenty-four to forty-eight hours, our five-year-old son was unconscious and in an oxygen tent; he remained unconscious for almost two days. One major confrontation occurred when the physician in charge suggested he might want to continue that experiment. When we refused to allow that to happen, the doctor threatened us with removal of all support, washing his hands of the entire matter unless we left the treatment program completely in his hands. The terrifying feeling that all of the medical support would suddenly be removed from our son was one that really caused parental stress and tension!

Instead of accepting the manifest failure of the experiment and concluding, in fact, that our youngster did need steroid therapy to control his seizures, the physician in charge introduced the interesting hypothesis that we, knowing that the experiment was going on, in some way communicated that to our son and caused the seizure to occur. He also, without any observable credentials, organized a group therapy session for parents, the effect of which was amateurishness and possibly damaging in the sense that it encouraged us to have guilt feelings about the way in which we were behaving or not behaving toward our child. The entire situation had to be resolved by getting a third party, in this case an eminent psychiatrist, to certify that we as parents were not emotionally disturbed and instead were showing signs of stress that were part of normal expectations given the conditions.

One of the mysterious factors, from a parental standpoint, regarding the professionals is why they consistently have difficulty in working cooperatively with one another to the patient's benefit. At one time, as we had become aware of the wide range of factors involved in the condition, we tried to bring together the relevant disciplines to create a single treatment program. This meant bringing together a triumverate of a psychiatrist, an endocrinologist, and an asthma specialist to see if they could agree on a single comprehensive treatment program. Our attempt to get such people together to talk was only a partial success; it took months before we could get a meeting. It is not encouraging for parents to see that professional roles, status, and internal conflicts get so manifestly in the way of benefits to their child.

Fortunately, this era of seeing the parents as the core problem has more or less passed and been replaced by an understanding that the handicap causes the parental stress; not the other way around. As the evolution of families has become more carefully studied, certain identifiable phases can be charted. One of those phases is that of the young family struggling to establish itself. It is a period of identifiable stress during which—in the typical nuclear family—the father is spending a great deal of time and effort to become established in his work, and the mother has one or more small children and feels the restrictions and limitations of her environment.

When one inserts a special problem or handicap into such a situation, then the stress and tensions are magnified. In our case, a simple example of such magnification would be whether the father in his role as professor would travel and, in effect, desert the family during a period of crisis, leaving the mother to deal with the issue alone. The issue "Is it safe to go?" was one that was constantly with us during the time that the senior author was traveling and establishing a professional reputation.

The Rest of the Family

There is always the concern that the siblings of the child in question will feel resentful of the amount of time and resources the parents invest in the handicapped child. Our knowledge of those dynamics has caused us to be specially concerned about the effect of Sean's illness on his relationships with his older brother and younger sister and brother. There was no way that we could prevent those feelings of resentment that there was an unfair distribution of time and resources among the members of the family. One can try to create special occasions, vacation trips, or other devices to help ease these feelings, but they will always be there. Perhaps the most useful strategy we used as parents in this situation was to openly discuss with the other youngsters, when they were old enough, how natural it was to be resentful and then to be mad at themselves for being resentful, since they knew why the parents *had* to spend extra time with the handicapped child.

Parentectomy

Perhaps the most difficult decision that we made as parents was to send our son to the Children's Asthmatic Research Institute and Hospital (CARIH), a special residential asthmatic treatment center, for eighteen months when he was twelve years old. After ten years of failure in attempting to help our son achieve an existence apart from steroid therapy, a physician whom we had come to respect and admire recommended that we seriously consider sending Sean to CARIH in Denver, Colorado. The thought of sending our son away for eighteen months, the minimum time allowed for treatment, meant reorganizing a close-knit family group, and that was not easily entertained.

Parents must also worry about rationalizing their own feelings about not wanting to send their child away for treatment, because many times they would feel better and freer if the youngster were away. We also came to realize how much a part of our lives he had become and what a gap would be left at his departure. Parents know that sons and daughters will leave home in late teens but not at twelve! This handicap, like most handicaps, causes a disjunction in the normal family evolution. The crucial factor in making the decision was the continuing and obvious effect that steroid therapy was having upon our son. His chubby cheeks and retarded physical growth had become too obvious to ignore, and the further possibility that his onset of puberty might be affected caused us to make the decision.

The residential hospital itself had many advantages, both medical and psychological, that seemed to have a positive impact on our son. One was the presence of immediate medical treatment before a seizure became difficult. Sean could, upon the first attack of asthma, go to the hospital and get immediate treatment and then go back to what he was doing. Instead of the long and painful toboggan slide that often occurred at home before we could get him to an emergency room of a hospital, he was able to determine his own treatment at his own timing.

In addition, the psychological atmosphere of CARIH was one of freedom and independence in which the youngsters controlled much of their own life situation. We were told they were to be as physical and active as they wished to be. If they wished to play football, they could play football. If, as a result of their playing, they had a seizure, they would go and get treatment and then return to the football game. This is such a dramatic shift from the inevitable situation in the home, school, or neighborhood where the youngster, upon the onset of the asthma, must stop and find some way of seeking treatment which is often delayed to the point where the treatment has to be much more severe and prolonged in order to deal with the problem.

In addition, Sean received psychological counseling at the hospital which allowed him to express some of the consequent fears he had that he never could share fully with us. The daily treatment program was designed around the most knowledgeable experts in a rapidly developing field where treatment sophistication was growing by the year and by the month. The rule that parents could visit only very briefly over that eighteen-month stretch and that the child could not go home was their attempt to maintain a treatment program free from the past habits and patterns that had turned out to be non-productive.

In many respects our experience as parents of a handicapped child was most atypical. One of the most unusual aspects of the story is that it has a happy and satisfying ending for the child and his parents. After his treatment program at CARIH, Sean returned free of steroid therapy, and physically mature, having grown a foot taller after having been removed from cortisone treatments. He was able to control and limit the occasional bouts of asthma that he still had. One of the proudest moments of our son's life, and ours as parents, was when Sean was able to participate on a state high school championship soccer team. It signaled to him his ability to master and conquer the problem and participate in activities that other youngsters admired and valued.

The Needs of Parents

Our experience, however, has taught us some things that we believe professionals should do to help future parents of youngsters like Sean. First, the professional staff should pay a great deal of attention to the need to counsel the parents on the consequences of the handicap, what they can expect to happen to them and to the family as a result of having a handicapped child. Such counseling cannot be done in a one-shot session, since the realization of the adjustments that have to be made come only gradually with experience. The need to bring the youngster for continued treatment of various sorts provides the ideal opportunity for such counseling sessions and should be made available to the parents if they feel that they can use and need it.

Some attempt should be made by a professional team dealing with chronic problems to explore support services that are available to the family. These would include examining the human support linkages of the family. Are there relatives or friends who can be helpful? Who can the parents turn to for support and help under conditions of stress and crisis? Professionals should assess that support network and supplement it where necessary with professional services.

Parents themselves need adequate knowledge of the range of support and treatment facilities for the disorder in question. It is a rare parent who has even the slightest knowledge of where to go or how to obtain the necessary resources to get help for his youngster. Although we were a professional family, used to dealing with the helping professions, many years passed before we felt we fully knew the range and kind of services that could be available to our son on a community, state, and federal level.

Our own academic training made it easier for us to gain access to university hospitals and to a variety of help from academic sources that is not available to the ordinary parent. Certainly, some general statement of the scope of treatment facilities available ought to be provided to the parents very early in the game so that they can invoke what options they feel appropriate for their situation.

It is in the best interest of both the parents and the professionals that the parents continue to play an active role in the treatment process with the youngster and not retreat, leaving the field entirely to professionals. If they do withdraw, and sometimes they are unwittingly allowed to do that when the professionals actively take responsibility for the treatment, then the treatment program for the child and family will almost inevitably suffer. We, as professionals, have gradually become aware of the outstanding resources that parents can be in the treatment program, yet the professionals still have a long way to go in awareness and fully valuing the parents' observations and sense of appropriateness of treatment for their child.

Parents, in a desperate effort to be helpful, often do as we did and invest in a wide variety of devices that some physicians might casually suggest. We bought dehumidifiers and humidifiers, placed electrostatic filters on our furnace, got air-conditioned houses and cars before it was popular, and at one time seriously considered replacing all our furniture and rugs with Japanese-type decor to reduce dust collecting in the house. This phase seems to be part of a parental desire to be useful, to play some important part in the treatment. Its unfavorable element is that if it is continued too long, it can add to a financial drain that already threatens the family.

There needs to be continuity of services for the family as the child progresses through various developmental stages. It is highly likely that many parents will have to deal with the problems of their handicapped child for the remainder of their lives. These parents need professional support and input as the child progresses toward adulthood. One of the most difficult times for the handicapped youngster is likely to be in adjusting to the unforgiving adolescent society of the secondary school. The child may have special problems of social adjustment and also may experience major concerns over an uncertain adult role that were not a factor in his early years.

The recent book, *Passages* (Sheehy, 1974), details the progression through some identifiable stages of various kinds of stresses and crises that an individual faces in the aging process. We need to be aware of the progressive evolution of the problems of the family with the handicapped child in a similar fashion and to create appropriate treatment resources for them throughout the span of life as necessary. We should not arbitrarily abandon or drop treatment because some point in time has been reached as when, for example, the public school education of the child ceases.

We have tried to avoid the human temptation, since the story in our case had an unexpected happy ending, to say that it all worked out for the best and that it was actually a strengthening and purifying experience. This would be utter nonsense. The strain and tension that was a part of our lives for fifteen years took its toll on us as individuals and as members of a family unit. It was not something that one would wish on other people, and the professionals should do their utmost to ameliorate these situations as much as humanly possible. Still, in one sense, there is a modicum of truth in the phrase from the popular song, "Without a Hurt, the Heart Is Hollow." We can never meet another family with a handicapped child and not feel a surge of empathy and understanding that would never have been present without our own experiences.

The final words of the article "Rejecting Parents?" still seem appropriate:

> The parents can be, and should be, valuable assistants in the training program of many kinds of exceptional children. A professional person who can understand and accept the reasons for the attitudes of parents, and also understands his or her own emotional reactions to the child and the parents, will be able to provide a richer and more effective training program for the exceptional child. (Gallagher, 1956, p. 294)

References

Gallagher, J. Rejecting parents? *Exceptional Children*, 1956, 22, 273–276, 294.

Sheehy, J. *Passages*. New York: E. P. Dutton & Co., 1974.